OVERCOMING
SEVENTH DAY ADVENTISM

Separating the Lies & Myths
from the Truth

LA SHAINE REYNOLDS

ILLUMIFY
MEDIA.COM

Overcoming Seventh Day Adventism

Unless otherwise noted, all Scripture is from the Holy Bible, New International Version®, NIV® Copyright ©1973, 1978, 1984, 2011 by Biblica, Inc.® Used by permission. All rights reserved worldwide.

The views and opinions expressed in this book are those of the author and do not necessarily reflect the official policy or position of Illumify Media Global.

Published by
Illumify Media Global
www.IllumifyMedia.com
"Let's bring your book to life!"

Paperback ISBN: 978-1-964251-47-9

Cover design by Debbie Lewis

Printed in the United States of America

Contents

Preface

I grew up in the Seventh-day Adventist Church. While there I was afraid, confused, and depressed. As far back as eight years old, I remember how the teaching of Ellen G. White kept me worried about my soul all the time.

There is so much wrong with what they teach and expect from their members. They believe in soul sleeping, meaning they don't even believe that believers who die go immediately to be with the Lord. Believers go to sleep until the resurrection. At that time unbelievers go to hell, but not for eternity. They believe in annihilationism, which means at some point unbelievers cease to exist.

Seventh-day Adventists are vegetarians and continue to uphold the Old Testament dietary laws. They claim that nothing was done away with (misunderstanding Jesus' fulfillment of God's law). They also teach that you must keep the law of Moses, especially the fourth commandment. This is where my fear and confusion came into play. I was told that if I didn't keep the commandment I would be judged and would not go to heaven. That was my constant fear. They also told me there was only one perfect person who walked this earth and did not sin and that was Jesus Christ. We can't be perfect because we are sinful humans. But you must live the perfect life and keep the commandments to get to Heaven. This is confusing even now, and I am an adult.

I lived in fear of God. I did not see Him as the loving, kind, and forgiving God that He is. I thought of Him as an angry God who was going to annihilate me along with the earth. I could not live the perfect life they teach. There was no hope for me, so I left the church depressed and defeated.

As you read this book you will be introduced to the two main pioneers who founded this religion, and I use the word *religion* because they stand on the fine line of being a church and a cult since what they teach isn't Christian.

This book isn't intended to put down the Seventh-day Adventist but to set things straight. I have very dear friends that still go to the Seventh-day Adventist Church, and I love them dearly. They are my brothers and sisters in Christ despite what that church teaches, and there isn't anything that would make me feel any other way. This is to help people who have been involved with the Seventh-day Adventist Church and are afraid and confused. It's for people who have come out of the Seventh-day Adventist Church and who feel alone. But most of all, it's to help any person who has been involved with any religion that has taught beliefs that do not line up with God's Word. And I hope it helps clear up any confusion and fear that one may have about God and His love.

CHAPTER 1

The Founding Pioneers

*"But about that day or hour no one knows, not even
the angels in heaven, nor the Son, but only the Father.*

—Matthew 24:36 NIV

Seventh-day Adventism had its roots in the Second Coming
movements of the nineteenth century. In 1818 William
Miller, a Baptist preacher, calculated that the return of Christ
would occur in 1843. When this proved wrong, he set the date
for October 22, 1844. Like many others, he based his prediction
largely on an exegesis of Daniel 9 and 12, using the erroneous
day-year equation (one prophetic day equals one historical
year). Tens of thousands of people followed Miller, and many
smaller groups branched off in this exciting religious climate, all
awaiting an imminent return of the Christ.

Following 1844, Miller stopped setting dates and acknowledged that he had been mistaken; many of his adherents went on to create Seventh-day Adventism.

James White, Joseph Bates, and others began practicing Sabbath-keeping in 1844, publishing their ideas in pamphlets. That same year people also followed the visions of the seventeen-year-old Ellen Harmon, who later became Ellen G. White. In October 1844 she claimed that God had shown her that Jesus had entered the holy of holies in heaven and the "investigative judgment," a key doctrine of the Adventist Church, had begun. She claimed to have a vision of Jesus investigating the books in heaven to determine who would be saved. She said that the mark of the beast would be taken on by the antichrist and claimed that it would be a curse to worship on Sunday and that anyone who obeyed the National Sunday Law would go to hell. She said those who worshipped on Saturday would be killed by those who went to Sunday worship. This is how the Seventh-day Adventists gained their name.

In 1846, Ellen White (1827-1915) and her husband, James, took the helm of Seventh-day Adventism. Between 1844 and 1951 she had two thousand visions compiled in more than 100,000 manuscript pages.

Though Adventist leaders always claim that the Bible is the only rule for their faith and practice, without Ellen White there would be no Seventh-day Adventism. Thus, the Advent movement is unbiblical since it was conducted under the leadership of a woman, which Scripture condemns (1 Timothy 2:12), and they set a date for Christ's return, which is forbidden in the Bible.

You may be thinking Scripture is wrong to forbid women to lead. What, then, is the apostle Paul's claim about women and teaching? He specifies men as elders (1 Timothy 3:1–7) and most probably as deacons (1 Timothy 3:8–13). The New Testament does not say that adult women can never be teachers of adult men. Priscilla and her husband, Aquila, in fact, did exactly that with Apollos, as recorded in Acts 18:26, and Phoebe served in some type of church leadership, with some suggesting that she may have been a deacon (Romans 16:1). But men are specified as the primary local church leaders, serving in the office of elders. In short, women were not meant to serve or lead in the specific ways in which the elder leads, even though women were not and are not excluded from praying in church gatherings where men lead.

As far as date setting, Jesus taught that nobody knows when He is going to come. Consider the following verses about date setting:

1. "But about that day or hour no one knows, not even the angels in heaven, nor the Son, but only the Father." (Matthew 24:36)
2. "So you also must be ready, because the Son of Man will come at an hour when you do not expect him." (Matthew 24:44)
3. "Therefore keep watch, because you do not know the day or the hour." (Matthew 25:13)
4. "But about that day or hour no one knows, not even the angels in heaven, nor the Son, but only the Father. Be on guard! Be alert! You do not know when that time will come." (Mark 13:32-33)

5. "He said to them: "It is not for you to know the times or dates the Father has set by his own authority." (Acts 1:7)

Ellen White was adamant that she "know the times or dates the Father has set by his own authority." [1]Jesus spoke literally when He said: "But about that day or hour no one knows, not even the angels in heaven, nor the Son, but only the Father. Matthew 24:36. By denying the plain sense of Scripture about the time and circumstances of Christ's return, the Adventists open the door to even worse false teachings.

The understanding of the Sabbath came about when Ellen White had her "vision" of the Sabbath day. This is when people started to accept her ideas and interpretations.

CHAPTER 2

A Little Girl Lost

My time in the Seventh-day Adventist Church started when I was seven years old. My Grandma Jones went to visit family in Florida and came back a member of the Seventh-day Adventist Church. I remember her telling Mom and Dad about getting baptized while she was in Florida. Before I knew it, we were going to the local Seventh-day Adventist Church and Mom and Dad were getting baptized. Now I want to take a little time to talk about my sweet grandmother.

Grandma Jones was very present in my early years. In fact, when mom was pregnant with me, she told her if I was a boy to send me back where I came from. Grandma had three boys. And I am sure that living with my dad and his brothers wasn't easy. So, I was the first granddaughter and to say Grandma was over the moon was an understatement. I was special and spoiled. She told my dad she wanted all granddaughters and that is exactly what she got: five healthy granddaughters.

I spent so much time with her and have many fond memories of her. I cherish them so much. She had breast and ovarian cancer. She ended up having a double mastectomy and a partial hysterectomy. But by that time, it had spread throughout her body. We moved in when I was seven years old so mom could help take care of her. After she was baptized, she seemed to get worse. She spent most of her time in bed. I was so sad and depressed. But I would do things to get her to smile and know that I loved her. I wrote her notes from me and my sister telling her we loved her, and I still have the note she wrote back to us telling us that she loved us too. My sister and I made a snowman outside her bedroom window so she could see it.

The days flew by, and it was time for me to start first grade. My first year in school went by fast. I loved my teacher, and I had a best friend. We went to church every Saturday. I remember feeling uneasy around the elders and pastors, and I just don't know why. It seemed that time flew by, but that is what happens when someone you love is sick and dying. Then the time came for me to start second grade. We were still living with Grandpa and Grandma, so mom could continue to care for her.

On a cold and snowy night in January, I was woken up to the cries of my grandpa saying, "My baby is gone." My sister and I slept on a sleeper sofa in the living room. Hearing Grandpa sobbing scared me. I knew Grandma had died. We were told to stay on the bed in the living room and not to move. But I had to see my grandma. I went to her room and stuck my head in the door. My dad was holding her hand, and his head was in his other hand; he was crying. I just turned around and went back to the living room. Now I was really scared because I had never seen my dad cry before.

Shortly thereafter the front door opened, and two men came in carrying a stretcher. When they came back out, they were wheeling out my grandma, who was covered in a sheet. I remember thinking she was going to get cold because of the snow. The next time I saw her was at the funeral home. As I looked at my grandma laying in her casket, my dad told me she was in a deep sleep. I remember feeling very confused. The question that came to my little mind was "If she was in a deep sleep, why are we burying her? "That was when my fear of death began. When I went in for minor surgery when I was little, the nurse told me I was going to be in a deep sleep. I was scared out of my mind. I was so afraid they were going to bury me. I feared death more than I should have at that young age and that fear follows me to this day. Sometimes I wonder if they used fear to get my grandmother to join the church.

As life continued, we became more involved with the church. And one of the main events we attended every year was the Daniel and Revelation Seminars. Back then they didn't provide childcare like they do now, so we had to sit with our parents during the presentation. The first image that struck fear into me was the dragon. The picture that was on the screen was the most horrible thing I had ever seen. It was red and its mouth was open, revealing sharp teeth. It's eyes glowed yellow, and I could not look away. I hated this more than anything. It just fed my fears. And that is what they wanted. To scare people so bad that they wouldn't forget. They teach and lead by fear.

The preacher was saying the dragon was the devil empowered by the Roman Empire. The papacy was the antichrist , and the beast would have great authority and power. Rome would usher in a national Sunday law, and they would put only Seventh-day Adventists to death because we didn't worship on Sunday. They taught that those who worship on Sunday would have the mark of the beast on their forehead and go to hell. And if you didn't live a perfect life and keep the Sabbath, you would go to hell. Try understanding that at eight years old. They had me paralyzed with fear. All I knew at the time was that I hated Rome and Catholics because they were bad people who were going to have me killed.

The Seventh-day Adventist absolutely instill fear concerning Rome, the Pope, and the Catholic Church. According to them every other denomination is hell bound because they do not follow the rules. They are prejudice when it comes to any other denomination, especially the Catholics. I have been told by a member that I have 666 already on my forehead and that I am going to hell. But they said they would pray for me.

I can't understand why they are so against Sunday, because that day is a very special day. It was a day when darkness moved away, and light and hope came out of a dark tomb. Our Lord and Savior rose on a Sunday. He died so we may have eternal life. He died before the Sabbath and those who loved Him spent a dark Sabbath mourning the death of their Messiah. I just have never understood that. How could Sunday be considered so bad?

Mom and Dad started implementing the beliefs at home. No going out or watching TV from sunset Friday to sunset Saturday.

We went on a vegetarian diet and were put into a Seventh-day Adventist school. I was cut off from the world. Those days were so lonely for me.

CHAPTER 3

Sabbath

"How much more valuable is a person than a sheep!
Therefore it is lawful to do good on the Sabbath."

—Matthew 12:12

E ach week as Friday approached, I got very depressed. I did
not want to go to church. I didn't want to sit there and have
someone point out my wrongdoings. I knew my soul was going
to hell because I had messed up so much during the week. And
some of the teachings scared me to death. Even as a child I knew
something wasn't right about the church. As I grew, I started to
see what was wrong. But I still thought that this church was the
only church that Jesus loved and that he was in the "Heavenly
Sanctuary" doing the "Investigative Judgment" of us.

It was pounded into my head that not keeping the Sabbath
was a sin. After all, it's one of God's ten commandments, they
told us. But there are other sins we commit many times every

day. We are called to repent of all sin. When you walk in sin, you are not walking in the will of God. You are not receiving God's best. They told us when the time of the mark of the beast came and Sunday worship would be enforced, the cowardly would take the mark. If you love God, then you must keep His commandments. This includes not letting your heart forget to keep the seventh-day Sabbath, they told us. Very soon the Sunday law would be an enforceable command. That would be the test of faithful devotion. Sunday is Satan's Saturday, we were told. It is the day set aside by Satan to keep the Sabbath. The Pope of Rome changed the holy days. He changed the Sabbath to Sunday. When Constantine made Christianity the law of the land, he made everyone worship on Sunday. The Sabbath is a memorial of creation and is an everlasting covenant. It was not to be changed by man. These fallen priests of Satan work for the devil and not God. Those who go to church on Sundays will be pardoned, but when worshiping on Sunday becomes a law, you will have to choose whether you will be standing with God or with Rome, Satan, and the Antichrist. And if you don't stand with God, you will get the mark of the beast.

The day of worship that Seventh-day Adventists go by is from sunset on Friday evening to sunset on Saturday evening. On Friday evenings I would sit in my quiet room wondering if the Sabbath would ever end. Saturday after church I would go into the woods behind my family home and sit in my favorite tree. It beat sitting in my room all alone just staring at the four walls. I began to tell myself that death would be better than going through this. And if you didn't show up for church, some of them would question you, wondering if you were sick or really working.

The church provided us with a card. It was a sunset calendar card to tell us when sunset began and ended. It was for the whole year. Dad explained how this card worked. On Fridays we had to be in at the time it said, and we could continue life as normal at the time the card told us on Saturday. The calendar card was by the telephone. Every time we used the phone, we had to look at it. Every time we got invited somewhere on Friday or Saturday we had to check the card. If what we wanted to do landed between the two times quoted, then we could not go. I hated that card! It ran our lives, as did the church.

From June through September, sunset occurs after 8 p.m. People get to finish their regular day's work hours before the Sabbath starts. Conversely, in November and December, when sunset might be before 5 p.m., they might work during some part of the Sabbath. Sometimes they could arrange with an employer to leave early on Friday evenings, so they can be home by sunset to prepare for the Sabbath. They could use some combination of vacation and personal time to leave work early during the winter months when the sun sets before the end of their regular shift. I can't tell you how many jobs I couldn't take or lost because of this. I would sit and wonder how a person could take care of their family if they can't work.

My dad worked different shifts, and not long after we joined the church, he went to working days. He told his supervisor that he couldn't work Friday evenings or Saturdays. The only way you were allowed to work those times was if you were a preacher, doctor, or nurse. No other jobs period. You weren't even allowed to cook on the Sabbath. You had to make the food for the Sabbath before the Sabbath. Housework, homework, shopping, watching TV, or whatever seems fit for doing on the Sabbath is considered work. If you are doing anything else than resting from work and worshipping God, and honoring God on the seventh day, you are being disobedient to God and treating your Sabbath and God with contempt. Generally, Seventh-day Adventists keep six days of work and then must rest in God, worshipping God, and honoring God, on the seventh day. I could not keep a job as a teenager because of this rule.

One Saturday my dad got sick, and he stayed home. The next week when we went to church an old man came up to my dad and asked; "Were you sick or was you working?" My dad was visibly upset, but he only told him that he had been home sick. I got upset because that man had no right to accuse my dad of working. It was none of his business what my dad was doing. That was between Dad and God.

I did not go to the Seventh-day Adventist school until I was in the seventh grade, so I had friends in the public school I went to. There were many times I was not allowed to do things with my friends because of the Sabbath. While my little friends were out playing, I was sitting in my room with just silence for company. If any birthday parties or school function landed on Friday or Saturday, which was always, my sister and I missed out because we had to observe the Sabbath. It was awful trying to explain to my friends why I couldn't do anything for those twenty-four hours. I know they probably thought I was a freak. It was so hard to explain why we observed the Sabbath.

We tried to do some of the activities the church provided, but it was too expensive. My dad worked at the paper mill, and he worked very hard to just put food on the table and clothes on our backs. There was hardly any leftover for snow skiing and camps and all the options the church provided. In fact, my sister and I were bullied a lot because our dad wasn't a preacher, lawyer, or doctor. We were considered beneath the other kids.

We were so lonely. My sister was a tomboy. She loved to be outside playing softball, climbing trees, and saving bugs and snakes. After we became Seventh-day Adventists, she couldn't play on the school softball team, and I couldn't be a cheerleader. We could read only the King James Version of the Bible on the Sabbath. The King James Version of the Bible is hard to read and understand as an adult. A child trying to read it is impossible.

As time went on, I got curious about the time of sunset and the days of the week. I thought "How in the world did they come up with Friday evening to Saturday as being the Sabbath?" There is not any Friday or Saturday mentioned in the Bible. What I found out was all these rules about the Sabbath comes down to one thing: we observed the Sabbath from sunset Friday to sunset Saturday because of Ellen G, White and Joseph Bates. She not only had a vision about what day to worship on, but she had a vision on what times the Sabbath would start and would end.

The understanding of the Sabbath came about when Ellen White had her "vision" of the Sabbath day. That was when people started to accept the ideas and interpretations of Ellen G. White, but Doug Batchlor says something different. In the YouTube video "Doug Batchelor Understanding Ellen White," Doug says the following:

"I was listening one night to another Bible answer program on the radio and someone said um they were asking about the seventh day Sabbath and somehow the word Seventh-day Adventist came up and this fellow who fancies himself a scholar he said well the seventh day Adventists believe the seventh day is the Sabbath because their Prophet Ellen White had a vision and saw a special halo around the seventh day and that's why they believe it's the Sabbath. I wished I could reach right through my radio speaker and take him by the tie and get his attention because nothing could be further from the truth."[2]

Ellen White said:

"In the Holiest I saw an ark; on the top and sides of it was purest gold. On each end of the ark was a lovely Cherub, with their wings spread out over it. Their faces were turned towards each other, and they looked downwards. Between the angels was a golden censor. Above the ark, where the angels stood, was an exceeding bright glory, that appeared like a throne where God dwelt. Jesus stood by the ark. And as the saints' prayers came up to Jesus, the incense in the censor would smoke, and He offered up the prayers of the saints with the smoke of the incense to His Father. In the ark, was the golden pot of manna, Aaron's rod that budded and the tables of stone which folded together like a book. Jesus opened them, and I saw the ten commandments written on them with the finger of God. On one table was four, and on the other six. The four on the first table shone brighter than the other six. **But the fourth (the Sabbath commandment,) shone above them all; for the Sabbath was set apart to be kept in honor of God's holy name. The holy Sabbath looked glorious—a halo of glory was all around it.** I saw that the Sabbath was not nailed to the cross. If it was, the other nine commandments were; and we are at liberty to go forth and break them all, as well as to break the fourth. I saw that God had not changed the Sabbath, for He never changes. But the Pope had changed it from the seventh to the first day of the week; for he was to change times and laws."[3] (emphasis added)

James White demanded that they don't budge from the time God gave "to us and Brother Bates." The Whites believed that God gave them the six o'clock time. Ellen White's "vision" of a clock pointing to 6 p.m. was enough to convince those inclined to believe her visions that the Sabbath started at 6 p.m. So, the Whites believed that God set the time at 6 o'clock. In fact, they believed it so much that James thought that any questioning about that time was the work of the Satan!

In the end, the Bible-based group's evidence became too overwhelming for those who believed in Ellen White's "visions" to be able to argue against it. According to Professor Baldwin, "Prior to the conference, [Bates] was still firmly committed to the 6:00 p.m. start time based on Ellen White's visions." According to John Andrews, an Adventist pioneer, "J.N." was commissioned in 1855 to study this subject and presented his findings at a conference held in 1855: "Joseph Bates, who was apparently wedded to the 6:00 p.m. position with the conviction that it had been confirmed by the vision of Ellen White, had been made chairman of the conference."[4]

Despite the presentation of biblical evidence and the fact that most of the participants concurred with Andrews, Ms. White persisted in insisting that the meeting should begin at 6:00 p.m. It is uncertain as to why, though.

At the conclusion of the conference, after most of the brothers had accepted the new start time, Ellen White experienced a vision in which she agreed with the new perspective. She was understandably upset, as she had been conversing with angels regarding the Sabbath for a period of almost a decade yet had not been informed of the correct beginning time. After the church had prayed for direction, she was presented with a clock which indicated that the Sabbath would begin at 6:00 p.m. in the evening. She was aware that some would doubt her prophetic ability. She was perplexed and asked her spirit guide for an explanation.

"I inquired why it had been thus, that at this late day we must change the time of commencing the Sabbath. Said the angel, 'Ye shall understand, but not yet, not yet.'"[5]

The spirit guide supposedly used the King James English "ye shall understand"; however, there is no evidence that Ellen

White ever understood this. To this day, the confusion persists. During the nine years in question, the Sabbath was the primary teaching of the closed-door Adventists, and numerous articles and tracts were written about its sanctity and the need to not work on the Sabbath. However, for nine years the angels did not inform Ellen White that she or Bates were violating the Sabbath when they worked on Friday evening after sunset or Sabbath evening before sunset. Finally, after Andrews, James, and the brethren concluded that the Sabbath began at sunset, Mrs. White's "angel" arrived to inform her that the Sabbath begins at sundown. This conversation would have been more persuasive had it taken place prior to the conference. As the saying goes, "better late than never."

The Old Testament law includes the Sabbath, but Christians are no longer bound by it (Galatians 4:1-26; Romans 6:14). Sunday, the first day of the week and the Lord's Day (Revelation 1:10), commemorates the new creation and the resurrection of Christ. The apostle Paul taught that each believer should make their own decision about observing a Sabbath rest: "One person considers one day more sacred than another; another considers every day alike. Each of them should be fully convinced in their own mind" (Romans 14:5).

I realized that we are called to worship God every day, not just on Saturday or Sunday. I have found some peace after I did this research. I would rather celebrate the day that my Lord comes out of the tomb than live a lie.

As for the Calander card, it ruled over my family's lives. But as soon as I was old enough to make my own decisions, that card went in the trash along with other materials that they give out. I hate thinking about that card. It upsets me that a piece of paper can have that kind of power over people. And it upsets me that people are being lied to and misled when the pastors, deacons, and elders know the truth.

The Investigative Judgement

We all know how it feels to be judged. Being judged can cascade into a range of psychological responses, such as anxiety, depression, and self-deprecation. When you are constantly subjected to judgments, perceived or otherwise, that erodes your self-confidence and makes you feel self-conscious of your behavior, sometimes to the point of stress and even long-term withdrawal or isolation, which can have a profound impact on one's mental health. I can remember feeling that way the whole time I was in the church. I was judged at school and at church. I was so miserable.

The Investigative Judgement cut me off, not just from mainstream Christianity, but from flesh-and-blood people in the real world. I was too young to make sense of the Investigative Judgment. I remember feeling watched all the time. At the SDA church school, I would get into trouble for stuff that I didn't understand. I would be punished for something but wouldn't know why. I had bad anxiety. I was always afraid I was going to do something wrong and displease God and not know that I was doing something wrong, that I was going to live through the last days because that is what I was taught. I would lay awake at night and worry about the second coming of Jesus and that I was going to hell. They preached on that and the Sabbath a lot.

The Investigative Judgment, or pre-Advent Judgment is not in the Bible; it is just something the Seventh-day Adventist think Jesus is doing now in heaven. Only Seventh-day Adventists teach the Investigative Judgment, which asserts that the divine judgment of professed Christians has been in progress since 1844 and that the works of all men and women written in "books of record" will show those who are authentic believers in God from those who are not. Those who have repented of sin and claimed the blood of Christ as their atoning sacrifice have become partakers of the righteousness of Christ and their sins will be blotted out. On the other hand, those who have not repented of their sins, their names will be blotted out of the book of life, and the record of their good deeds will be erased from the book of God's remembrance.[6]

Many Adventists have shied away from discussing their misgivings about the Investigative Judgment for fear that they will unsettle the membership. For me, Investigative Judgment has been a mental torment. The Investigative Judgment is a mere philosophical band-aid to cover up the error of 1844. Here are some key points about the Investigative Judgement:

1. It's an extra-Biblical doctrine invented entirely by Ellen White.
2. It cheapens the Reformation gospel of Salvation by grace through faith.
3. It removes from Adventists the certainty of salvation and replaces it with endless terror.

4. Throughout the history of Christianity, not a single denomination has found some kind of use for this doctrine, and so none of them have embraced it.

5. Most Adventist pastors and theologians know in their hearts that the doctrine is bogus, but they don't dare admit it.

I was so scared when I heard about this. I imagined God standing behind a podium with a great book opened. He would read a person's judgement while looking at them, and He looked at an angel and point to the side and the angel would grab the person and drag them to the side where hell was and throw them in. It was terrible because teaching like this would give me nightmares. I worried every single day for years, and it still bothers me on some days. I just wanted to touch on this because it is such a big part of the Seventh-day Adventist doctrine and belief.

CHAPTER 4

School

"If anyone causes one of these little ones—those who believe in me—to stumble, it would be better for them to have a large millstone hung around their neck and to be drowned in the depths of the sea.

—Matthew 18:6

School days are supposed to be times of joy and sadness, first loves and first kisses, parties, and the senior prom. I started the Seventh-day Adventist school when I was in the seventh grade. It was very different than the public school I attended. There was not any after school sports because of the Sabbath. I did have a few teachers I loved, but the principal was so mean and cruel. He made fun of the kids and would play very cruel jokes on them, and he would encourage the other kids to join him. I was at the center of his cruelty. He taught my class, and one day I raised my hand to answer a question. I got it wrong, and he took that opportunity to laugh and make cruel remarks about me and encouraged the class to do the same. I never raised my hand again.

One day he came into class and announced that a brother and sister who attended the school would not be going there any longer. Their mother had died, and their father had taking them out and placed them in public school. He told us we had to get down on our knees and pray because they we going to a terrible school. He made it seem like their souls were lost, and they would never get to heaven. They had no chance of being saved. So, we were on our knees for about twenty-five minutes praying, and I remember not knowing what in the world to think. It terrified me. This principle let everyone know you would go to hell if you went to public school. When I got out of the SDA school system, I finally could breathe easier. When. went back to visit once, it was apparent that I was no longer one of them. I never was anyway. It was the first time I realized how cultic the SDA church is.

Another time that stands in my mind very clearly was when I went to the bathroom at school. It was after school had ended and most of the students left. I needed to go to the bathroom, so I turned around and went back. I walked into the girl's bathroom and looked in the mirror. There was a pair of men's feet. My eyes went wide, and fear gripped my heart. Then I heard the principal ask who was there. I ran out of the bathroom and ran to the end of the walkway. When I composed myself, I walked back toward the bathroom, and he was walking toward me. He asked me if I had seen anyone come out of the girl's bathroom and I said no I hadn't. I didn't tell anyone about that incident until almost thirty years later. I never felt comfortable being around any man in the church.

When I was in the eighth grade and going to the SDA school, I was very depressed. My depression started when I was younger, but it got worse when I started the SDA school. I was so depressed that I was planning to kill myself. The day I was planning it one of my classmates came into the bathroom. I was just standing there trying to fix my hair. She could see that I was distressed. So, she came up and fixed my hair for me. She showed me such kindness that day that I decided not to kill myself. I do believe that God sent her to me. After that I made friends with a couple of other girls. We do keep in contact today. I love them dearly and there isn't anything I wouldn't do to help them if they needed it.

At the age of thirteen I was approached by the pastor of the church and told I needed to be baptized. He made it sound urgent, and it kind of scared me. They try to get the kids baptized young. They do not believe in baptizing babies, but when one hits thirteen, then you need to be baptized. So, I went to the classes to study the Bible, Ellen White, and the last days, which was being shoved down my throat at that time. Getting off the subject right quick, this is how backwards they really were. When the girls hit eighth grade, we had to take etiquette class. Yes, we did. That was so boring! I already knew how to sit and talk and bake. I am a southern girl. My mom started teaching me when I was five years old. I could make buttermilk biscuits by the time I was eight. I did not need the class.

After elementary school I attended a year at the academy. That's when I faced a violent incident at school. The kids made fun of me, and I stayed depressed. I felt so out of place. This boy that attended the academy relentlessly bullied me. One morning I was on my way to class when he backed me up against a tree. He blocked me from leaving. He got into my face, pulled out a knife, and told me if I ever caused him trouble, he would kill me. Then he moved away, and I hurried off to class. I was afraid the whole day, but I finally got the courage to go to the principal and tell him what had happened. The principal didn't do anything to that boy. You see the boy and his family were generational Seventh-day Adventist, which meant their whole family had been a part of the church for generations, so they were important people in the church. As I said before, my dad wasn't a doctor, lawyer, or preacher. Therefore, I wasn't important. I was just another kid whose parents were willing to pay tuition, and they gladly took it.

I stayed on my guard, and I stayed around other people, so he didn't have the chance to corner me. But it didn't take long before they suspended him for good for doing it to another girl, a girl whose family was a big deal in the church. This is where my feelings of worthlessness came into play. I thought if I wasn't worth anything to this God-fearing remnant, how could I be worthy to God?

The rules of the school, as you can imagine were very strict. No one of the opposite sex was allowed in our dorm rooms. No jeans except at work. No jewelry, no makeup, no holding hands or kissing, and above all, no mixing with the public-school kids. And you had to work a job they picked out for you, so you could help your parents pay the school bill. Your parents' status in the church determined what jobs you got. The poor kids worked in the cafeteria or school maintenance. The rich kids worked in office related jobs or nursing homes. Of course, my best friend and I got cafeteria jobs. We spent more time working jobs at the schools than we did in class.

Looking at the other girls at the academy, they were so much prettier, and the boys treated them more nicely. I thought I was ugly. In fact, the boys made fun of me. I had glasses and braces. I had a health problem which in turn caused me to have a spiritual problem. I think more bullying goes on in the Seventh-day Adventist Schools than they are willing to admit.

I still tried to fit in as best as I could. There was a dinner planned for us kids one night, and I went even though I didn't have a date. I ended up sitting with a guy who I had a crush on. After dinner they set up a movie in the gym for us. During that film the boy kissed me, and it was my first kiss. That was not allowed. Well, the other kids saw it, and by the next day I had kids pointing and laughing at me. They made terrible remarks. I was so embarrassed. Even my boss at the cafeteria laughed at me and made rude comments while I tried to work. It was not that special moment that every girl had.

Another instance just about cost me my life. The school took us all to a lake nearby to swim and have fun. We were told to stay close to the bank and not go out to the little island. The year before a boy from the school took his girlfriend to the island and ended up drowning. I did not want to be there. You could feel the darkness around that place. I was standing on the pier looking out over the water and a boy came up and pushed me in. There are weeds all around that pier. I got tangled up in them. When the boy and some other students realized I wasn't coming up, the boy jumped in the water and pulled me out. As I was sitting there wet and haggard looking a guy from the yearbook came up and took a picture. I begged him not to put it in the yearbook. He said he wouldn't. When the yearbook came out that picture was in the center of the yearbook. I just cried because I thought I could trust him. I should have known better.

They punished me mercilessly. Looking back, I realize how all of it was tied to how bad my mental health was. I think their education was subpar. All the tuition goes to the greedy conference leaders. Those schools are a scheme, so they can continue to indoctrinate generation after generation of kids and keep them in the Adventist bubble. Maybe you had the same dark experiences growing up in SDA. If you have had any experiences like this go get help. If you have experienced abuse and trauma under the guise of the church, you have a right to be heard, understood, and believed.

I felt lonely at school. All my friends from elementary school had left except for my best friend. In fact, she went to the academy with me for two years. She wasn't happy and neither was I. But it was nice to not be happy with my best friend. At the end of our ninth-grade year, she moved to Florida. Her uncle didn't like it that we went to school until noon and from noon until 3:00 we worked. When she left, I went to dad and begged him to put me back into public school. And so, I started my tenth-grade year at public high school. But this wouldn't be the end of how the Seventh-day Adventist school system would touch my life.

I was excited to go to public school. Mom and Dad relaxed the rules of not doing anything on the Sabbath. I didn't stick out so much at the public school. I was with kids whose dad's worked at the Paper Mill with my dad. Most of the mill workers even grew up together. All of the stress of living under the rules and fear led to an eating disorder that still followed me back into public school. I still worried about my salvation; God scared me so bad.

Even though I was in public high school, I still went to church. I turned sixteen years old when I started public school again. It was awesome. One night at church a deacon and another man who were church members was outside. I went to the car to get something and when I turned around, they were standing there. The deacon asked how old I was, and I told him I had just turned sixteen. He grabbed me and whipped me sixteen times. Then the other man did the same. They hit me so hard that I had bruises and handprints on me for quite some time. I tried to run from them, but they caught up with me. I didn't tell my parents because I knew it wouldn't do any good.

I loved being with kids who didn't judge and bully me for what my dad did for a living or for how long my family had been in the church. In the public school I was with normal teenagers, if there is such a thing, doing normal teenage things. I went to Friday night football games and out on dates. There were dances and the prom. The most awesome thing I did was order my high school ring, The Seventh-day Adventists don't want woman wearing jewelry, except for a plain wedding band. They didn't like for the women to wear jeans or makeup. But that's what I got to do when I started public high school. It felt so good to be free. And I got to listen to pop and rock music. The music of the eighties was awesome! And going to see horror movies was my favorite thing to do. There were a lot of great movies in the eighties also.

The most exciting time of any teenage life was graduation. I was excited. I had my senior pictures made, ordered the name cards, invitations, and my cap and gown. I was looking at colleges and making plans for what the next stage of my life was going to be. Two weeks before graduation I got called to the counselor's office. I had no idea what was going on. I sat down, and the counselor told me I wouldn't be graduating because I needed two more credits. I sat there stunned. When I got home, I told mom and dad what was going on. They went to the school the next morning and found out that the Bible class I took at the private school did not count. Dad asked if the Bible could be considered a history, but they said no. So, I did not graduate. I never walked across that stage, nor did I receive a high school diploma. Instead, I got a GED. But I still went to school every day until the end of the year. So, yes, I did finish twelve years of high school. They couldn't take that away from me.

CHAPTER 5

Harmful Diet Restrictions

Everything that lives and moves about will be food
for you. Just as I gave you the green plants, I now give
you everything.

—Genesis 9:3

The Seventh-day Adventist dietary laws, and that is what they are, have caused some very dangerous health risk. To this day I still have to deal with the effects of the diet. And they will follow me for the rest of my life.

I hated the vegetarian diet. I have nothing against vegetarians. I know it is a healthy diet if done the right way. You see, Seventh-day Adventists live by what Ellen White said in her books *Healthful Living* (1897–1898), *The Health Food Ministry* (1970), *The Ministry of Healing* (1905). White wrote extensively about health, nutrition, and vegetarianism in her book *Counsels on Diet and Foods*. She gave advice on what foods to eat and how to eat them in moderation. She warned against using tobacco, which at the time was medically acceptable. She opposed eating meat and spicy foods—even though she ate them herself—and she was against drinking alcohol and smoking, as well as medications and doctors. She was a cult leader who made rules for the people but didn't follow them herself.

The Seventh-day Adventist church teaches that we need to eat a healthy plant-based diet of fruits, vegetables, whole grains, nuts, seeds, and legumes, but all members aren't vegetarians or vegans. SDA members are permitted to eat whatever they choose (most of them do). But the vegetarians judge the ones who eat meat, and a self-righteous leader of a particular congregation can choose to enforce the rule. My family was in the church that specifically said eating pork could send an Adventist to hell. Pork, shellfish, scaleless fish, any scavenger or bottom feeder (catfish), caffeine, alcohol, and any meat from any animal without a split hoof was forbidden.

The following is what Ellen White taught about meat in the diet:

- Clouds the brain
- Benumbs the intellect
- Enfeebles and deadens the moral nature
- Weakens the higher powers
- Lessens spirituality
- Renders the mind incapable of understanding truth
- Causes insubordination
- Stimulates lustful propensities
- Strengthens the lower passions

- Animalizes a person by strengthening the animal appetites
- Interferes with the religious life
- Causes a person to miss out on companionship with heavenly angels
- May cause God to decide not to heal someone's sickness
- Causes sickness and disease
- Endangers physical, mental, and spiritual health

The most outrageous statement that Ellen White made is when she states eating meat is a deprivation of spiritual development.[7]

When my family joined the church, we changed our diet to follow its dietary laws. It was hard for me. I had already had problems from when I was a baby. I was allergic to whey, although we didn't know that at the time. I hated the food. I was sick all the time. Everything we bought couldn't be high in sugar or have sugar substitutes, food additives, or animal fat. I bought cookies for a potluck and was told by one of the women they couldn't serve them because they had animal fat in them.

Everybody in the church must maintain a healthy weight and lifestyle. To be overweight and sick not only meant you had a health problem, but that you had a spiritual problem as well. Each person represented the health message. When I got sick as a teenager, I knew I had a spiritual problem

I was never a heavy girl, but I had to watch what I ate. This is what led to my eating disorder. I compared myself to the other girls at the academy; they were so much prettier, and the boys seemed to pay more attention to them. The boys made fun of me. I had glasses and braces. To try to make myself prettier, I started making myself throw up when I ate. I also took diet pills. I would hide them under my mattress.

Even though I wasn't overweight, I didn't want to get fat because if I did, my spiritual life would be taken away. I went from 115 pounds to 90 pounds; it was a very troubling time for me. We went on a class trip and stopped at Burger King. I ordered a whopper. One of the girls said, "You don't want the meat, do you?" And I said, "yes, I do." She gave me the most awful look. I just knew I was going to go to hell.

When I ate anything that had sugar in it, I would cry. If I ate anything that was forbidden, I would make myself throw it up. It got to where I ate one meal maybe every two to three days. You could see my ribs through my skin. I looked like a skeleton with skin stretched over it. Even after I went back to public school, I didn't change my eating habits. In fact, I grew even more restrictive. I was depressed and found myself unable to go out to eat or even to any social event because I was afraid of eating. And if I did eat, I would go throw up and ask for forgiveness for eating something I shouldn't have eaten. It wreaked havoc on my body. I didn't realize how much damage I had done to my body until I wanted to have kids.

All I ever wanted was to be a mom. I couldn't wait for the day I could hold my little gift from God in my arms. When I got married, and we decided to have a child, I noticed that my periods were irregular if I had them at all. I just thought my body was just different. Then one night I went to the ER with a migraine and before they gave me pain meds, I had to have a pregnancy test. It came out positive. I was over the moon. But my happiness didn't last long. About a week after I ended up having a miscarriage. It broke my heart. My eating disorder caused me to have a hard time getting pregnant and carrying it to term. I am happy to say that I did have a precious baby boy. It was a hard pregnancy, and I just about lost him when I was seven months pregnant, but God blessed me and gave me an amazing son.

I still suffer the effects of my eating disorder today. I have osteoporosis. At fifty-five years old I have the bones of an eighty-year-old. I have broken my tail bone, fractured my hip, and cracked my pelvic bone. I also broke my ankle on both sides. I had to have a plate, and four screws put in and that's when they discovered how bad my bones were. The doctor told my mom that the surgery took longer than expected because my bones were paper thin, and they had a hard time attaching the hardware. I have broken my knee and my wrist. Every time I cough bad, I more than likely will break a rib. COVID was not fun. I have anemia and digestive problems and suffer from a weakened immune system. I also suffer from bipolar, depression, and anxiety.

There is a new type of disorder called orthorexia nervosa. It is an unhealthy emphasis on good nutrition. Good wholesome foods are great, but when you have orthorexia, you get so hung up on it that it ruins your whole health. It's not even an official diagnosis. People with this mindset think that most food items as not "pure" enough. By the time they are older, orthorexia sufferers tend to refuse entire meals that aren't as good as they'd like, or which they don't prepare themselves. The secret to beating it is realizing that though eating healthy is good for you, how you're doing it is killing you. You have to retrain yourself to think differently about it. Adventists had to make sure the medications they were prescribed stayed in line with the healthy living that Ellen White had laid out. It meant for me that I stayed sick because I wasn't getting what my young body needed to stay healthy. And being sick was a sin.

I truly believe that God provides for us physically, mentally, and spiritually. And God knows what His children need to keep them healthy and well. God puts medications and doctors here to help us. Just like He did when He threw Adam and Eve out of the garden. He didn't let them die immediately. He provided for them, and He provides for us. I don't like to think about animals having to die for us. But God put them here for us, and He guides doctors to help His children, like with insulin. My question to the Seventh-day Adventist is this: Would you deny your child the medication they need to keep them from dying, or would you follow the insane rants of a woman who was sick herself?

One more thing that I would like to add is concerning endometriosis, a chronic condition where tissue similar to the lining of the uterus grows outside of the uterus. I suffered most of my life with it. Of course, the people at church told me to take all these herbs and drink a special kind of milk. I did what they said, and it got worse. I finally went to the doctor, and he went in to take it out. When I woke up, he told me that it had started turning black and that was the last stage before cancer. If I had listened to the church and not went to the doctor, I probably would have died from cancer. I thank the Lord for pushing me to go to the doctor when I did. I ended up having to have a hysterectomy at the age of thirty-two.

CHAPTER 6

Faith and Ideology

I will bless those who bless you, and whoever curses you I will curse.

—Genesis 12:3

"You shall not murder."

—Exodus 20:13

In my research of dietary restrictions, I ran across something that sent chills through me. People don't know this. I don't know if the conference knows this and is just not telling people. I have a feeling they do. This is why the Seventh-day Adventists don't teach anything about WWII.

Nazi Germany posed significant challenges for small denominational churches. When Adolf Hitler ascended to power, the German Seventh-day Adventist, like most Germans, knew that Germany needed a strong leader. Hitler appeared to be a suitable choice. His personal lifestyle choices—such as abstaining from tea, coffee, alcohol, and meat—aligned with Adventist values, so they regarded him as a potential savior. It is important to highlight the consequences of these decisions. After the war the church's support of Hitler resulted in disgrace for both the German denomination and the global Adventist community.

Before the war, in the Adventist community of Friedensau, Germany, an overwhelming 99.9 percent cast their votes for the Nazi Party. While the Adventists expressed a desire for a strong Führer and generally supported Hitler, their level of support was not uniform. Some in the church were concerned with Hitler's conflicting statements regarding religious freedom, despite the Nazi Party's opposition to it. M. Busch, the departmental secretary of the South German Union Conference, openly endorsed Hitler and cited his assertion in Mein Kampf that "for the political Fuhrer all religious teachings and arrangements are untouchable."[8] The Adventists perceived Hitler as an advocate for religious matters. However, the Nazi Party's program included point 24, which claimed to support positive Christianity without aligning with any specific denomination. This ambiguity sparked debate among Christian groups as to the true meaning of "positive Christianity" remained unclear. Ultimately, when Hitler assumed dictatorial power in Germany, the discourse surrounding this contradiction ceased, and it soon became evident to Christian groups what Hitler meant by "positive Christianity."

In 1935, the privileges that Adventists had previously enjoyed, including the observance of the Sabbath, the sale of religious literature, necessary financial transfers for missionary activities, and certain publications, were prohibited. This situation prompted German Adventists to reevaluate their stance on the separation of church and state and the principle of religious liberty. They recognized that Nazi Germany was facing significant criticism internationally due to its treatment of smaller denominational churches, particularly those with roots in the United States. If these smaller denominations were prepared to assist in enhancing the Nazi regime's image abroad, the government was inclined to grant them some degree of leniency. This marked the beginning of the German Seventh-day Adventist denomination compromising its integrity and fundamental principles. The denomination collaborated with German authorities to foster a more favorable perception of Nazi Germany in the United States to secure improved treatment domestically. This initiative was facilitated through the Adventist welfare program.

The welfare system established by the Seventh-day Adventists was regarded as the most effective in Germany. Their approach to welfare distinguished the Adventists from other organizations. Through this system, the Seventh-day Adventist Church was able to demonstrate its commitment to Christian values and its patriotic allegiance to the state. While the Nazi regime appreciated the contributions of the Adventists, they objected to the terminology used, opting to replace "Christian" with "heroic." Consequently, the Adventist welfare initiative was integrated into the National Socialist People's Welfare

Department. This integration conflicted with the Adventists' principle of maintaining a separation between church and state. Nevertheless, the German Adventists embraced this incorporation, believing it would enable them to achieve greater outcomes and assist a larger number of individuals. However, this alignment with the state required the Adventists to adhere to laws that prohibited welfare assistance to Jews, individuals deemed anti-social, or other undesirables. Additionally, the Adventists unilaterally decided that members of the Seventh-day Adventist Reform Movement would also be excluded from receiving aid. As a result, rather than extending their support to more individuals, the Adventists ended up discriminating against those who were most in need. Alongside their welfare initiatives, health reforms and racial hygiene became increasingly significant.

The Adventists believed that along with their welfare program, their health ideals were leading the way for a new Germany. Adolf Minck, soon-to-be president of the German Adventist Church, said, "We are not unprepared for the new order. After all, we have helped prepare the way for it and helped to bring it about."[9] The problem with supporting the Nazi government in their health program was the government's belief in the principles of Darwinism. The Adventist's denominational stance was against Darwin's principles. The German Adventists sacrificed this principle for the Nazi government. To gain favor with the Nazi government, the Adventists changed what was written in their publications and reformed their health message. The Adventists "frequently print[ed] negative comments about the Jews. They also tried to show that even though the

Adventist's teachings about the Sabbath seemed Jewish, they were not Jewish. The Adventists also believed in the sterilization program. Direct statements and the reprinting of non-Adventist articles showed their support for sterilization. The mentally weak, schizophrenics, epileptics, blind, deaf, crippled, alcoholics, drug addicts – all were to be sterilized. 'This law,' an article in the Seventh-day Adventist paper Jugend-Leitstern said, was 'a great advance in the uplifting of our people." [10]

The stance of German Adventists shifted from a focus on *caritas*, which emphasized caring for the vulnerable, to a belief in the elimination of the weak as part of God's work. This transformation led them to adopt a völkisch ideology, which was a belief in German superiority and even a spiritual resistance to the evils of industrialization. The Adventists established a highly organized and effective welfare system that was particularly adept at collaborating with state authorities. This framework enabled Hulda Jost, **director of Adventist welfare and the leader of the Adventist Nurses Association,** to gain recognition from the Nazi regime.

Hulda Jost managed several nursing homes and supplied staff to numerous hospitals across Germany. In her role, she forged connections within the Nazi government and beyond Europe. A staunch supporter of Hitler and his policies, her relationships proved crucial in helping the Adventist denomination endure during the regime's early years. This made her an ideal candidate to travel to the United States to represent the Nazi government.

Jost's journey to the United States was scheduled for 1936, coinciding with the General Conference quadrennial session in San Francisco. She received an invitation from the Adventist headquarters in Washington, DC, and her travel itinerary was coordinated between the Adventist headquarters and the German Ministry of Public Enlightenment and Propaganda. Arriving several months in advance, Jost toured the United States to discuss German welfare services.

Upon her arrival, Jost met with J. L. McElhany, the vice president of the General Conference, and her interpreter, Louise C. Kleuser. She also had a meeting at the German embassy, where she was advised to steer clear of political issues and focus solely on the accomplishments in social services. Jost highlighted Germany's achievements under Hitler to various Adventist and other organizations. However, issues began to surface regarding her lectures in April.

The challenges escalated during Jost's time in Denver when she alienated a significant portion of her audience by excessively discussing Hitler and the Jewish issue in her lecture. The Adventist leaders perceived her talks to be propaganda for Hitler and his regime. While still in Denver, the administrator of the Boulder sanitarium approached Jost, requesting that she confine her lectures to the gospel, as they were not interested in hearing any propaganda related to Hitler. Following her lectures in Denver, the General Conference decided to closely monitor Jost's activities. Although the General Conference viewed Jost as a potential liability by the end of her lecture series in the United States, her mission to correct the distorted image of Germany had been fulfilled.

Jost and the German Adventist leaders felt they had fulfilled their responsibilities in the United States, hoping for a more lenient stance from the Nazi government toward their denomination. However, while they were abroad, the German government enacted a new decree. They mandated that all school children attend school on Saturdays, which prohibited Adventist children from studying the Bible in class. Some soldiers were no longer able to keep the Sabbath. In response, Jost wrote a letter to high-ranking officials expressing her concerns about the decree. She highlighted the Adventists' support for the Nazi government and her efforts in the United States to enhance their image. Joseph Goebbels even sent a letter to the Reich Ministry of Church Affairs, but the decree remained in effect. This instance illustrated that despite Hulda's connections and the trip to the United States, the Adventists did not benefit. However, other situations demonstrated the advantages of having a powerful ally.

One notable instance involved the gestapo's investigation of nurses affiliated with the Adventist Nurses Association who had been dismissed on the grounds of being deemed politically unreliable. Jost expressed her discontent regarding their termination and questioned the accuracy of the gestapo's findings. Consequently, she sought assistance from her acquaintances in the Ministry of Public Enlightenment and Propaganda to investigate the matter. The subsequent report from the Propaganda Ministry concluded that the nurses were politically cleared. Another instance highlighting Jost's connections occurred in 1937 when a friend within the Ministry of Church Affairs who had ties to the gestapo alerted her to impending plans to disband the Adventist denomination. Through her network, Jost was able to reach out to senior officials in the gestapo, successfully thwarting the initiative to dissolve the denomination.

In March 1938, Hulda Jost passed away, believing that her efforts had contributed to the survival of the Adventist denomination during the initial years of Hitler's regime. While in the United States, Jost was aware that her message that the Nazi's respected liberty of conscience and the complete religious freedom enjoyed was untrue. Nevertheless, she held the conviction that her various efforts and compromises with the Nazi regime would shield her denomination from gestapo harassment. Due to Jost's connections and actions, the Adventist denomination became increasingly intertwined with the state. Although the Adventists upheld the principle separation of church and state, Jost's actions contradicted this belief. Despite the numerous compromises made in the early years, the Adventists found themselves without any security from the Nazi government. Lacking protection from the Nazi regime, the Adventists continued to make concessions to the regime.

The Second World War commenced with Hitler's invasion of Poland on September 1, 1939. In the preceding year, the Adventist denomination began the process of eliminating "Jewish words" from its practices. The term "Sabbath School" was replaced with "Bible School," and the word "Sabbath" was substituted with "Rest Day." Following the onset of WWII, the government enacted a regulation prohibiting pastors from collecting offerings in churches or through house visits. A loophole in this regulation, however, permitted pastors to levy fees on their members, which enabled smaller denominational pastors and churches to endure during the early stages of the conflict.

In Germany, Adventists maintained their support for Hitler and his regime. They were influenced by publications from the late 1930s that portrayed Hitler as a strong national figure who supported reclaiming its former territories. They believed that God was guiding the war and reassured to readers of Adventist journals. Michael Budnick, the president of the East German Union, communicated to other conference leaders that Adolf Minck had been apprehended by the gestapo for failing to adhere to Sabbath work restrictions.

Church leaders concluded that for the survival of the Adventist denomination, it was essential to issue a directive on April 30, 1940, instructing pastors that "in total war there can only be total commitment and sacrifice."[11] The challenge of total war was the leaders' desire to avoid a repeat of the schism that had occurred during World War I. To mitigate this risk, the circular also directed pastors to educate their congregants on their scriptural obligations, emphasizing that one of the core beliefs of Adventists is that the Holy Scriptures represent the word of God.

The document indicated that, based on biblical principles, church members were expected to submit to military forces, citing the command: "Submit yourselves, for the Lord's sake to every authority" (2 Peter 2:13). In addition to this, the German Adventists also invoked Romans 13, which addresses the obligation of individuals to submit to governmental authorities to rationalize their ongoing support for Hitler and his regime. W. Mueller, the president of the East German Conference, has been quoted as stating: Under no circumstances did any Adventist have the right to resist the government, even if the government prevented him from exercising his faith. Resistance would be unfortunate because it would mark Adventists as opponents of the new state, a situation that should be prevented.[12] This illustrates that German leaders were reluctant to oppose the Nazi government, as they did not wish to be perceived as adversaries of the regime. These leaders needed to avoid creating disturbances within the Nazi framework, even when the policies of the regime conflicted with their denominational beliefs. The German Adventist leaders overlooked or neglected the principle that their primary submission should be to God and His authority rather than to secular powers.

This circular appeared to be effective. In 1940, the government issued a report identifying the religious sects permitted to operate peacefully due to their focus on religious teachings. The Seventh-day Adventists were among those sects listed. Nevertheless, this designation did not provide a sense of security for the Adventists, who continued to make concessions to the Nazi regime.

The German Adventists maintained their support for Hitler and his regime throughout World War II. Many Adventists served with dedication in the military, predominantly in combat roles, and advanced within the ranks. This practice contradicted the denomination's principle that participation in warfare should be limited to non-combatant roles. Church leaders asserted, "the pastors and members of our Church stand loyally by their Volk and fatherland as well at its leadership, ready to sacrifice life and possessions." While they expressed a willingness to sacrifice their lives and belongings for their country, they did not extend the same commitment to their religious convictions.[13]

I am sure there were other religions that also supported Hitler and his regime. The thing about the Seventh-day Adventist is that they talk about how in the end times people will hunt them and kill them for their religious beliefs. They helped put millions of Jews to death by turning a blind eye all for the sake of wanting a strong leader. They already had a strong leader, God. When all is said and done, because Adolf Hitler permitted them to keep their Sabbath, most Adventists did not rebel against the Nazi regime.

The reason I included this is because my sister and I became close to some of the Holocaust survivors. One thing they told us was, "Don't let anybody forget." We promised that we would make sure that their family's story would be told. And I intend on keeping that promise

CHAPTER 7

Heaven and Soul Sleeping

*Then he said, "Jesus, remember me when you come
into your kingdom." Jesus answered him, "Truly I tell
you, today you will be with me in paradise."*

—Luke 23:42-43

B illy Graham played a big part in my spiritual life. When I
was a little girl, I would sit with my grandma and watch his
crusades. It was such a special time. Even though I was going to
the Seventh-day Adventist Church and was only eight years old,
I enjoyed listening to him. Billy Graham's sermons and all the
people that came forward at the alter call amazed me. The song
"Just as I am" is very special to me. What I was feeling at that
time and didn't understand was the Holy Spirit.

When I became pregnant with my first child, I was so happy.
I have always wanted kids. But it wasn't meant to be. I had a
miscarriage. I was so upset, and I really didn't know what to

think. All I knew was that I lost a precious gift from God. I wondered if I would see my baby one day. I went to one of the deacons at church to get answers. I asked him if I would see my baby in heaven. He told me, "No you won't because it wasn't old enough to make a decision to follow God." In other words, it hadn't reached the age of accountability. It floored me, and I was so upset. I couldn't believe that my precious baby wasn't in heaven. That I wouldn't see it. I started asking different people and pastors their opinions on it. All the answers I got were that I would see my baby one day. I know God is not that cruel. My baby was an innocent life just like all children, and I know I will see my precious baby one day.

I read a comment on a Seventh-day Adventist website once. Someone asked about children who die. Do they go to heaven? A woman answered her, "No they do not. It's not like heaven has children running around up there." My mouth dropped open. No one has the right to say that to a parent who has lost a child. Nobody has the right to go to a person that has lost anyone and say things like that. This kind of thinking makes me hate going to funerals. It's bad not only because I've lost someone I love, but because it takes me back to my eight-year-old self and what I was told about my baby later. They make me afraid and angry. I really had a hard time during the pandemic because I lost five family members and two friends. It was a very dark and fearful time for me. But with God's help I came through it.

Do I believe that you go to heaven when you die? Yes, I do. There are just too many people who have had near-death experiences, including me, where they've seen heaven. Hospice patients have reported seeing angels and Jesus and loved ones before they die. I think that the Lord does this so that the person will not be afraid.

When I was nine years old, I had to have my tonsils and adenoids taken out and tubes put in my ears. The nurse told me I was going to be in a deep sleep. And yes, I went wild. They had to medicate me so I would calm down. Anyway, it seemed like a minute, but the next thing I knew I was floating and watching the doctor work on me. I remember the light being so bright. I saw my Oscar the Grouch doll next to me. He had a mask and hat on. Then as fast as it happened it ended, and I woke up. I didn't tell anyone about this until I was an adult. So, yes, I do believe we go to heaven.

How can someone tell a child that he didn't go to heaven and seen Jesus when a child in a totally different country sees Jesus and paints what He looks like, and they both agree that is what Jesus looks like? How can you tell someone who is dying that they are not seeing angels, Jesus, or loved ones? There is just so much proof that one goes there when they are done here. I've included a list of movies and books at the end of this book that are amazing, and I really suggest that you read and watch them.

I read an article from *Proclamation!* the online magazine of Life Assurance Ministries. that interviewed Doug Batchelor on the death of Billy Graham. What he said was so disrespectful not only to us who think highly of Graham as God's messenger, but to the Graham family also. He said the following:

"Graham will thank me for giving you this real quick study. The Bible is very clear: people do not go to heaven until the resurrection, and they do not go to heaven until the judgment."

Hear you can see how they put down other denominations and pastors of other denominations. To me it sounds like Doug Batchelor is judging. It makes me wonder if he is jealous of Billy Graham. Billy Graham had a true gift from God. He brought the Word of God to people all around the world. And now his sons and grandson are following in his footsteps. I can remember sitting with my grandmother watching his crusades on TV. It's a very special memory for me.

My questions to Doug Batchlor are this: How can you say that someone doesn't go to heaven when we have had so many people have near-death experiences, including me? There are too many people who have been to heaven and back, including children. So, what are you going to do? Tell a child that it was all in his imagination or that they dreamed it? And how do you know what Rev. Graham would want you to say? And if you don't go to heaven when you die, how did Moses appear with Elijah to Jesus before He was crucified? I'm sure that the Seventh-day Adventist would have an answer. I don't ever remember in all the time I was there that they ever talked about Moses and Elijah appearing with Jesus.

The Seventh-day Adventist believes in soul sleeping, the idea that a person's soul "sleeps" after death until the day of judgment and resurrection. The Bible does not support the idea of soul sleep. The Bible does not imply actual slumber when it speaks of someone "sleeping" regarding death. The state of a dead body appearing to be asleep is only a description of death.

I had dreams about the second coming of Jesus several times. The first time I dreamed that an angel came down and picked me up. We only went halfway up and then the angel sat me down and said, "I will come back and pick you up." It scared me to death. In the next dream I was at my grandfather's funeral, and he sat up in the casket. I looked at the window, and there was a very bright light. I woke up scared to death. I know that Jesus doesn't want me to be afraid of His second coming. I try to remember that, but these dreams only made me scared of Him. It also made me think that God was a very mean God. And that is what the Seventh-day Adventist teaches. They control by fear!

It's depressing to sit and think about dying and not going to heaven. When my grandpa died in 2022, I stared at his coffin at the graveyard, and all I could think about was him "sleeping." I imagined him in that box waking up and him being trapped underground with all the dirt on top of him. I about lost it. I would go to his grave and just sit there. I don't know why. But all I could think about was him in that box in the ground. My wonderful husband was there to be my support. And I know I will see my grandpa, family, friends, and most of all my baby one day. I always have to remind myself that becoming absent from the body is being present with the Lord for those who follow him (2 Corinthians 5:8).

The COVID pandemic was very bad for me. I lost five family members and two friends. That was a dark time for me. I questioned if God was really with me, and I told myself I wasn't going to heaven. I got scared and questioned my faith. I would lie on the couch and talk to the Lord and tell him what I was feeling. And I thought I was losing my faith. I finally realized that I wasn't losing faith if I was praying to Him. God wants us to ask the hard questions. I realized I was going through a season and that God loved me and was there with me.

My Grandpa Jones attended the Seventh-day Adventist church before he passed away. But he was also a member of a Baptist church. When time came for his funeral, they had a preacher from each denomination there to give the eulogy. The elder from the SDA church went first. He said that Grandpa was in a deep sleep and when the day the Lord comes, he would rise from the grave. The Baptist preacher was next. He told us that grandpa was in the presence of our Lord and Savior. And one day we would be together again. Then my aunt got up to read a poem and made the statement that she believed that grandpa believed that he was going to heaven, not sleep in a box in the ground. Talk about awkward. Now, I find myself giggling when I think about it. Only in my life would this happen.

CHAPTER 8

The National Sunday Law and the Mark of the Beast

During the 2024 election, the Seventh-day Adventist put out an article stating that Donald Trump signed an order requiring all Americans to worship on Sunday. They said those who failed to abide by this order would be arrested and sentenced to ten years of hard labor. This happens every election year. Every president is going to bring the national Sunday law into effect. When asked about this, President Trump said: "Seventh-day Adventist I don't know about."[14] They have done this every election year.

Seventh-day Adventists (SDAs) preach that a national Sunday law will one day be enacted in the United States. They believe the First Amendment to the US Constitution will be overturned, and we all will be required to make Sunday a sacred day. Once the law passes, SDAs will be prosecuted for refusing to see the first day of the week as sacred. They teach that only the SDA Church will be tortured and eventually put to death.

Seventh-day Adventists believe the Roman Catholic Church is the first beast in Revelation 13. Since the Bible says that this very beast will attack the saints of God and destroy the world with false worship (Revelation 13:5-8), they teach that the Catholic Church will attack those who observe the seventh-day Sabbath of God. They teach that the Roman Catholic Church replaced the second commandment with one that moved God's Sabbath from Saturday to Sunday. They take this attack on God's law as proof of the authority of the Seventh-day Adventist Church.

SDAs believe that the mark of the beast will come when there is a national Sunday law, which will demand that we all observe Sunday as a sacred day. The second monster of Revelation 13 is the United States, according to the SDA. They imagine that the Roman Catholic Church and Protestants in the US will "swim" together at some point to enact a national Sunday law. If combined, these two powers will impose a Sunday law across all countries.

Ellen White said when "'America, the nation of religious freedom, shall join with the pope in indoctrinating the conscience and compel men to observe the [Catholic Church's] false Sabbath, all the people of every nation in the world shall be influenced to imitate her.' She added: 'The decree forbidding the sanctification of this day [Sunday] is to go forth to the whole world. . . .' Trial and persecution will befall all who do according to the fourth commandment, not worship this false Sabbath."[15] Finally, SDAs teach that the passing of a national Sunday Law in the US will result in a "time of trouble" for the entire world.

Their view is that God will put all men to the test to see if they will succumb to enslavement of Rome's false Sabbath and acquire the mark of the beast. Their vision is that God's saints will defy these laws by holding fast to their faith and by keeping the fourth commandment, which makes the seventh day of the week holy. So, there you have it. Another fear tactic they use on people.

As a child the church would have the Daniel and Revelation seminars, now called Amazing Facts, every year. I hated that time of year. I would have to sit through these videos of some very scary creatures. The preacher would talk about the beast in Daniel and show pictures of what they looked like. I was scared to death. I was just eight years old the first time I went to these seminars. They would give me nightmares. The one that scared me the most was the dragon. The preacher was telling us that this beast was the Pope, and he would usher in the national Sunday law. We would be killed because the Pope wanted to murder us and only us. I would sit there and imagine being killed. Every year, I would beg God not to let the beast come and don't let anyone kill me. This caused me to have anxiety, fear, and depression at the age of nine. I never slept well because I didn't want to dream about these creatures. In my dreams I would see the lion with eagles' wings; a bear with ribs in its mouth; a leopard with four wings and four heads; and a beast that had iron teeth, brass nails, ten horns and a little horn that came up in the middle and got rid of three horns. But the beast that really gave me nightmares was the dragon in Revelation. The dragon was huge and red. It had seven heads and ten horns. It was the scariest thing I had ever seen.

One night I dreamed that there were flying animals around me. I was so scared because they had come to take us to hell.

I woke up in tears and sweat. Even now and then that same fear comes over me. The preacher told us that the people who worshipped on Sunday will kill us by chopping off our heads or hanging us. I didn't trust people around me and I was always watching the news waiting for the announcement that the national Sunday law was in effect. A little girl worrying about this kind of stuff is wrong. They mentally abused me is what they did. One preacher told me I had demons inside me, and he had to pray with me at the altar. It was terrible Being up there with the preacher and the elders of the church with their hands on me asking God to get rid of demons. That made me feel as if I were the most terrible little girl. I grew up thinking I was worthless and that I was going to go to hell. I should have been running around playing with friends and playing with dolls. Instead, I was busy trying to be perfect.

The preacher would yell and ask us "Are you going to die for God or have 666 on your forehead and turn your back on God? You will die if you side with God!" We were told that we would go to hell twice. How that is possible, I don't know.

A false belief can destroy a family and even your belief in the true God! Ask them whether they personally know Jesus or whether they are confident of their salvation, and you'll be amazed at how different the responses are. It's not about a relationship but about going to church on Saturday. These people are obsessed with waiting for the Sunday law, and very obsessed with the Sabbath. These scary tactics damage people. I can't tell you how many marriages I have seen break up because of this abuse. Even today I still have problems with my mental health because of this. There will be times when I tell my husband that I am not going to heaven. I still struggle today. I am in counseling for it, and I have been for years. I am having to deprogram myself of what I was taught. The national Sunday law does only one thing and that's to makes people afraid. It makes me so sad to sit here and know that there is a child out there suffering just like I did. I'm convinced many would leave Adventism if they weren't so afraid.

One day I sat down in my office and was just looking up the national Sunday law and ran across a website that horrified me. I couldn't believe that they had gone this far. This is nothing but child abuse plain and simply.

Camp Au Sable is a Seventh-day Adventist camp in Michigan. For the most part there are a lot of typical camp activities for kids—horseback riding, archery, and swimming. But some of their lessons borderline on abuse. In 2011 the staff and counselors put on a "last days" event where they impersonated soldiers and the chased kids through the woods with make-believe guns. If caught, the children were forced to kneel and choose whether they would "die" for the Sabbath or not. It was horribly traumatic. You can see the pictures online of this taking place.[16] It gets worse. The church would be filled with people and "soldiers" would storm the front door. The people believed it was real and that it was the end of the world. This is messed up on so many levels. It's a miracle with all the school and church shootings these "soldiers" didn't get shot. They were playing a dangerous game. I was wondering if they had security in place, and it dawned on me that these men were probably their security people.

The SDA believes that in the last days there is a probation period when people can still be saved. Let me explain what probation according to the church means. For them Probation started when Satan and his angels rebelled. And people can repent of their sins, confess them, and receive grace and forgiveness. Probation ends when the person dies because they can't make decisions to change and repent. Once the probation has ended all the plagues from Revelation will start falling on all the "Sunday keepers." Apparently, that will make us Sunday keepers mad, and we will proceed to arrest all the Adventists and kill them. They say that the SDA would need to plant their own food to survive. And whoever is on medication cannot buy their medication because they wouldn't have the mark of the beast. This is what they honestly think. Can you imagine living every day believing your friends and family were going to murder you and your kids any minute? This is their way of thinking. In SDA eschatology these things are always just around the corner. If you screw up and fail probation, then you'll be cursed and start killing your family as well. I can tell you it's a horrifying, dreary mountain to climb.

No, Sunday worship is not the mark of the beast. Sunday is a day of remembering. Christians go to church on Sundays to remember Jesus Christ's resurrection. Christians rejoice that God is with us not only on Sunday but every day of the week, by the power of the Holy Spirit.

This second beast, the papacy. motivates the people to construct an image of the first beast, the dragon, (Satan) and make it come alive. People will need to worship that image, or they'll be killed. Furthermore, the second beast will require all men to have a mark on their right hand or forehead. It is not about going to church on Sunday. It's about being children of God that refuse to give allegiance to the enemy.

As I was doing a Bible study recently, I ran across this passage:

> As I urged you when I went into Macedonia, stay there in Ephesus so that you may command certain people not to teach false doctrines any longer or to devote themselves to myths and endless genealogies. Such things promote controversial speculations rather than advancing God's work—which is by faith. The goal of this command is love, which comes from a pure heart and a good conscience and a sincere faith. Some have departed from these and have turned to meaningless talk. They want to be teachers of the law, but they do not know what they are talking about or what they so confidently affirm. (1 Timothy 3-7)

We do not know what sort of false teaching Paul was referring to here, but we do know that the addition of anything (such as man-made regulations) to the message of God's grace nullifies the death of Jesus on the cross. But one thing I do know is that the Seventh-day Adventist will go to great lengths to hide their secrets.

Consider for a moment what would happen if America became overwhelmingly Seventh-day Adventist. What do you believe would be the most significant law to pass in the legislature in a very short period of time? A Saturday law would be approved, which is exactly contrary of what they think is the mark of the beast. I have no doubt that Adventists would insist that everyone observe the seventh day of the week and worship god in accordance with their rules. Anyone who did not follow with great zeal would be murdered because of their beliefs. Just something to think about.

CHAPTER 9

The Rest of my Story

My life was not normal. After I left the church, I was so depressed and anxious about the second coming of Jesus. I was worried about being forced to take the mark and all I would have to face during the tribulation. I feared death and worried about being perfect. Because of these things I tried to go back to the SDA. But every time I walked through the doors of the church, I felt judged and like I was worthless. My depression and fear became almost unbearable. But I had to remember that the preacher and the other members were not perfect—no matter how much they wanted to portray to the outside world that they were.

I married my first husband when I was nineteen years old. He was an alcoholic and was physically and mentally abusive. When I done something, he didn't like, he slapped or whipped me. Yes, he whipped me. It was in this marriage that I got pregnant and lost my first child. When I had my miscarriage, he was so happy. I couldn't believe how happy he was at the doctor's office. This marriage came to an end when he told me that I couldn't talk or see my family again. I never looked back. I felt relieved, but I also felt guilty because I let my marriage get bad, and I went through a divorce. I made two very bad mistakes according to the church. I married someone outside the church, and I got a divorce. Now any man I married would be considered an adulterer and that was a big no in the church.

My second marriage was to a less-than-ideal husband. He never helped me out around the house, and he was a big mamma's boy. Before we got married, he had to get his mother's permission. It was during this time I had my son. I him my miracle baby because at seven months pregnant I just about lost him. They had the helicopter ready to take him to a hospital. But they got my labor stopped and I was able to carry him to term. Anyway, with my husband and my baby, it was like having two children. Our marriage failed because we were separated for long periods of time. He was in the military and word got back to me that he was with another woman. I don't know if that is true, but one thing is for sure, I was not going to put up with that stuff.

I figured since I wasn't going to heaven, I should have some fun. I started smoking, drinking, and staying out all night. I was doing everything that the SDA church told me not to do. I also got mixed up in Wicca. This is a form of witchcraft. I was trying to find a place where people would accept me for who I was and not judge me. Thanks to my father in heaven, I got out of that real fast. It was such a dark place. That time in my life was dark and depressing.

My third husband was also an alcoholic. He was so bad that it affected his liver. He worked the third shift (11 p.m. to 7 a.m.)

and would start drinking when he got home from work in the mornings. When he was off, he would drink all day long. I had to do everything around the house. I cooked and cleaned and did yard work outside as well as work a full-time job. Again, not an ideal husband. Another failure in the eyes of the church and God.

After I left the church, I worried about my eternal life. In fact, I went back a couple of times thinking that maybe just maybe I could live a perfect life. That was wishful thinking. In fact, a lady at the church who I'll call Jan told me I needed to get out of my job at the casino. They had me thinking that I had to quit my job to be part of the church. So, that's what I did. They wanted me to be a substitute teacher while the teacher was out at the school. I don't have or ever had a teaching degree. But that didn't matter to them. They just didn't want me working in a casino. In fact, there were a few jobs the church wanted me to quit.

I worked at the casino for a while and though I didn't like it, I had to provide for me and my young son. It was there that I got the shock of my life. I worked in security for the casino and one of the jobs was to walk around and make sure people were behaving. As I walked toward the back of the casino, I ran into one of my former SDA pastors. He was as shocked to see me there as I was to see him. He had the "deer in the headlights" look. I said hi and asked him what he was doing there. He told me he was there to have a Bible lesson with a woman in one of the restaurants. I knew that was a lie, but I went along with it. I said my goodbyes and went about my work. Later he came up to me and told me the truth and said, "Please don't tell anyone I was here." I just said OK.

There was a time when he was there and didn't know I was watching him. His game of choice was blackjack. While I was looking around the slot machine one night one of my coworkers came up and asked me what I was doing. I told him that my former pastor time was at the blackjack table, and I explained the SDA beliefs to him. I pointed him out and my coworker told me, "I know him. I had to escort him out one night because he was hitting the table very hard, and he was angry." The tables were computers and not real cards. So, if the table got hit hard enough it could destroy the computer. It blew my mind.

At this time, I had gone back to the church. One day I walked through the door and right there in the foyer was a display of VHS tapes of the pastor and his family singing. He was selling them to make money. This worried me a lot, so I asked Jan about the display. She told me the pastor had falling on hard times, and they were letting him sell video tapes of his family singing to help him out. She also went on to tell me that the church had paid some of his bills. I had to tell them what was going on. I couldn't let them give their hard-earned money to him, so he could gamble it away. I told Jan what I knew, and she went to the new pastor and told him what was going on. When the old pastor came to pick up the money from his videos, the new pastor took him into the office and told him he couldn't sell his videos there anymore and that they couldn't help him with money anymore. I felt so bad for lying to him when I said I wouldn't tell, but I couldn't let them continue to give him money. This same pastor was accused of sexually harassing a woman. He was let go from his duties. I don't even know if he is still going to church. The church didn't even offer to get him help even though they have multiple mental health doctors in the Advent Health system. It's a sad thing when they don't practice what they preach.

After I left the casino, I went back to my job as an assistant manager at a local restaurant. I had to sneak around because I worked Saturdays. I couldn't let the church know, or I would have been put down and pressured to quit. It was hard for me because I had to take care of my son, and I didn't want God to hate me. I can now say that God wants us to take care of the precious gifts that He gives us in our children and family.

Jan and her husband would come to order food and expect to get a discount. I would put the order under my name on the employee meal list and go without eating. She and her husband would do the same at a department store where a friend worked. They expected him to give them discounts when they bought clothes. It was terrible. I personally felt if I didn't give them what they wanted, I would be put down and ostracized.

It didn't take me long to leave the church for good. I couldn't take all the restrictions and being put down over every aspect of my life. I was called a liar, an adulteress, and was told I was going to hell. When they found out about me being in Wicca, I had to get rebaptized, and one man was so angry that if looks could kill I would be dead. I lost a lot of friends. Some still at least talk to me; others don't even want to see me. That used to bother me a lot. I felt like a failure and that God hated me. Most of the church turned their backs on me. Even today if I run into a member, I get terrible looks, and they turn their backs and walk the other way. As for my family, they came out a couple of years after I did. My dad still believes in some of their ways. We don't talk about it because it gets heated fast. It had already ruined part of my life, and I didn't want it to do the same with mine and my dad's relationship.

After my third divorce, I took time to heal myself mentally and physically. I got help for my depression, bipolar, and anxiety. I needed to take the time to get healthy. I began walking with God again, and it was amazing. I had a great job and a great apartment. I started going to the church that I grew up in. It was a Baptist church, and the members welcomed me with open arms. Some of the members know four generations of my family. They watched my dad and me and my son grow up. It was like going back home. I felt welcomed, loved, and not judged. But the SDA teachings haunted and followed me.

Time went on and I met my husband, Tim, in October of 2006. Yes, he gave me permission to use his name. I was so lonely being by myself, and I told God that I was so lonely. It wasn't long after I prayed that Tim came into my life. The first thing we shared with each other was our faith walk. We tell people that we are the original ninety-day fiancé. We met in October, got engaged in November, and got married in December. I know that was fast, but it felt right.

I didn't tell him about my time in the SDA church until later. We were at home one night, and I was at the computer. I started telling him about the church and what I went through. I told him how wrong other religions were and how the SDA believed that all people except the Seventh-day Adventist would receive the mark. I told him about how the SDA members would be put to death. He looked at me like I was out of my mind. I told him people didn't go to heaven when they died. He told me that what I said was not biblical and to show him in the Bible where it said that. I got very angry and picked up a vase and threw it. He patiently and lovingly told me to study and read for myself.

My life hasn't been an easy one concerning my beliefs. I ask every pastor I meet if I am going to heaven. But it's not only the pastors. I also asked some of my professors, and they all say the same thing: If you truly believe that Christ is the Son of God and that he died on the cross and rose the third day and have asked for forgiveness for my sins, then I shouldn't worry. I also have a terrible time being perfect. I must stop and remind myself that I can't be perfect like the Seventh-day Adventist preached. We are humans and Jesus was the only perfect one that walked this earth. And if we could live perfect lives, then he wouldn't have had to die for us. I feel sorry for those in the church. They must lead a terrible life. It drives me crazy some days.

After some time, I got in touch with two of my friends who went to the private school with me. I found out that they had left the church, so I started talking to them about everything that was bothering me. They left for similar reasons. I asked them how to get the teaching of the church out of your head. They both told me to study the Bible, and one of them told me, "You have to read your way out of it." This advice helped me so much. I felt as if I wasn't alone. It was at this time that Tim told me, "You need to write a book, so you can help others." For ten years he encouraged me and stood by me. Finally, I said OK. I know that writing this book is going to upset a lot of people in the SDA church, and I will probably lose some friends. But if I can help one person, it will be worth it. I am not going to let their teachings rule my life anymore.

I don't blame the church for my three marriages ending in divorce. But I do blame them for putting so much fear in me that I rushed into relationships I probably would have never sought in the first place. God has blessed me so much. On days that my past comes back to haunt me, I remember the blessings and remind myself that I can't go back and change it. I also remind myself that the Lord has forgiven me of those sins. And I must keep my eyes on Him and keep looking forward, or I will stay stuck in the quicksand of life.

I had to go to counseling to get deprogrammed. I did intensive psychotherapy and confrontation therapy to eliminate the conditioning and reclaim my free will. It's been a long hard road, and I still have more work to do. And I realized that God answered my prayers about giving me kids. Not only did he give me my miracle son, who is amazing and wonderful, I got five amazing and wonderful bonus kids when Tim and I got married. I always wanted a boy and a girl. Now I have five boys and one girl. Tim and I also have five awesome and smart grandkids. I couldn't ask any more of my heavenly Father except to take me home to heaven with Him.

Do the end times still scare me? Yes, it does. I have done a couple of studies on Revelation, and don't feel as scared. Now I am more in awe at what God has in store for us. Some days there is a war inside my head, and that is exactly what it is. A war because the enemy will use everything, he has against a person to make them stop following God, feel unworthy, and to instill fear. In any situation like that I remember my favorite Bible verses.

Do I think that the Seventh-day Adventist is a cult? The SDA church's ideas are far-fetched and dangerous for many. They teach false and destructive doctrines that were created by a false prophet. Ellen White was a very sick woman. They have had just over one hundred years of false information given to them and to admit this would be admitting disloyalty to their "prophet." So, are they a cult? I believe they are.

What do I believe now? I believe that God loves me and that His Son died on a wooden cross so that I could spend eternity with Him. God loves us no matter what. We are not perfect, nor can we be. Only one person that walked this earth was perfect and that was Jesus. I believe when we die, we go to heaven. There is too much evidence out there that says we do. I do believe that there isn't anything I can do to make God stop loving me. Do you stop loving your child when they do something wrong? Of course not. We may not be happy with their choices, but that would not cause us to stop loving them. Just as God isn't happy with his children's choices at times, He still loves us.

What advice would I give to someone who is coming out of the Seventh-day Adventist Church or who has family in it? My advice is what my friend said, read yourself out of it. Study the Bible and ask God for guidance as you read it. Get yourself a good study Bible and read it without Ellen White's writings. Find a good church that doesn't push ridiculous ideas and talk with the pastor. As far as family and friends being in it, you must love them through it. Send them a text or drop a note in the mail. Don't let them forget that even though you don't agree with them, you still love them and will be there for them always. I still have friends in the church that send me stuff about the church through the mail or texts. I do smile when I see it because I know that they love and care for me or they wouldn't be sending me this stuff. I still love those people very much. They are my sisters and brothers in Christ.

Am I upset and angry? I am not upset with Ellen White because she was a sick person who as a child got hit so hard in the head it put her in a coma. She had a traumatic brain injury, and since she worked in her dad's hat making business, I have no doubt she had mercury poison. (Back then they used **mercurous nitrate**, a form of mercury, to cure the felt used in hats.) I am angry with the leaders now because they know the truth, and still, they are spreading lies and making people afraid of a God that is amazing.

And as for Tim and me, our relationship and marriage are still going strong. I tell people that I can see God's hands all over this marriage. I truly believe that God also sent Tim to help me through this. We talk about the Bible and pray together. We keep God at the center of our relationship, and we ask Him for guidance. My walk with God has gotten stronger. I love Him so much.

Believers who struggle with sin and acknowledge their mistakes and seek God's forgiveness and transformation are showing signs of true faith. The Bible emphasizes that genuine salvation changes our hearts, leading us to love what God loves and detest what he detests. It is not enough to simply claim faith; our actions must align with a sincere love for God above all else. In the same way King David was deeply troubled by his sins, a true believer is always conscious of their wrongdoings and strives to follow God's will. Therefore, take time to examine your heart and where your priorities lie. Ask yourself, "Is my life centered around God, or am I consumed by worldly pleasures?"

Authentic faith results in a life transformed to honor God in every aspect. Do not be misled by the temporary pleasure of sin; instead, draw close to God, confess your sins, and aim to live a life that truly reflects your love for Him. Only then can you find assurance in your place in His kingdom upon His return.

Writing this book has been healing for me. I cried, got angry, and cried again. I am doing good for the most part. I find peace in knowing that I am a child of a King who loves me and fights for me. He will never leave me. I have an amazing church family who is ready to help if something is bothering me. I have also learned that you can be friends with other people of other denominations. Just because you believe differently doesn't mean you can't be friends. In the end we all are made in the image of God. I look up every day to see if He is coming. I look around and see God's beauty in a very sinful world. Time is getting short. My prayer is that you trust God and go to Him first. Read His word and talk to Him. But most of all ask Him into your life and admit that you are a sinner that needs to be saved. Give your life to God, because at the end of the day, He is the only one that matters. May God bless and keep each of you in His loving arms.

Appendix

Below is an excerpt from an article by Pastor Sydney Cleveland, former Pastor of the Seventh-day Adventist Church and Robert K. Sanders, former elder and thirty-seven-year member of the Seventh-day Adventist Church. I chose to include questions that correspond with what I wrote in the book, but you can go and read the whole article if you are interested. I have included the myth, which is what Elle G. White said, the truth, which is what the Bible says, and the lie, which is what the Seventh-day Apologists say. The number of the question will be beside it so you can find it in the list in the article.

ELLEN G. WHITE CONTRADICTS the BIBLE OVER 50 TIMES[17]

By Robert K. Sanders

"There is one straight chain of truth without one heretical sentence in that which I have written."

— **Ellen G. White, Letter 329A, 1905.**

"If what a prophet proclaims in the name of the LORD does not take place or come true, that is a message the LORD has not spoken. That prophet has spoken presumptuously. Do not be afraid of him."
(Deuteronomy 18:22 NIV)

Ellen White was one of the founders of the Seventh-day Adventist church back in the middle 1800s. She claimed to receive communications from God through visions, dreams, and angelic visitors. Though long dead, Seventh-day Adventists continue to claim Ellen White was a genuine prophetess, and they commonly refer to her as "the Lord's Messenger" to Church.

The original document, "Examples of Ellen White Contradicting the Bible, was written as a direct challenge to Ellen G. White's followers to compare her writings to the Bible. Seventh-day Adventists are fond of quoting Isaiah 8:20 (KJV): "To the law and to the testimony: if they speak not according to this word, it is because there is no light in them"—mark it carefully, this text did not say there is some light in them, it said "there is no light in them!" Now, on the basis of Isaiah 8:20, let us see if Ellen White agrees with the supreme definer of truth: the Bible. If she does, then there is truly "light" in her. If she does not agree with the Bible, then she is a false prophet leading Seventh-day Adventists into utter darkness."

This list of contradictions is compiled by Pastor Sydney Cleveland, former Pastor of the Seventh-day Adventist Church and Robert K. Sanders, former Elder and thirty-seven-year member of the Seventh-day Adventist Church.

What to look for in the apologist's rebuttal and our reply.

1. What we quoted was truly what EGW actually said and wrote; therefore, Ellen White's apologists cannot claim we misquoted her. So there is agreement among us that she actually said the things we have quoted.

2. Because Ellen White may have agreed with the Bible in one section of her writings does not excuse her for contradicting the Bible in other parts of her writings. Since Ellen G. White repeatedly contradicted herself as well as Scripture, she repeatedly fails the test of a true Bible prophet.

3. When faced with Ellen White's many contradictions of Scripture and contradictions of herself, apologists argue: "you have taken EGW statements out of context." So the question you, the reader, must first decide is: have we have taken her statements out of context, or have her apologists taken them out of context? We have always included the full references with each statement we quote so readers can study each one in context. We

are confident the evidence clearly demonstrates to our readers that we have told truth!

4. The apologists at Ellen White website call us "D&D" to "protect our identity." We have never hidden our work under the shadow of anonymity. Instead, we have always had our names clearly published as the originator of this document, and we publish our names on our respective web sites. No one has ever had to wonder who we are. However, Ellen White's apologists apparently are ashamed of their work, for they do not have the courage to list their names or backgrounds as of this writing!

5. In their rebuttals, the apologists have at times used many words and circular arguments in order to confuse the issue. To paraphrase King Solomon: "many words are found in the speech of a fool" (Ecclesiastes 5:3). We have presented facts in the briefest, clearest possible manner.

The SDA Church agrees that the cannon of the Bible closed two thousand years ago with the book of Revelation. They also tell us that Ellen White's writings are not an addition to the Bible but are just as inspired as the writers of the Bible. This concept, both in theory and practice, makes EGW's writings equal to the Bible as far as the average Seventh-day Adventist is concerned. By their accepting Ellen White as a prophetess and "messenger of God," they unwittingly open the cannon of the Bible. In this they are no different from other cults who likewise proclaim the prophet supremacy of their leader(s).

Note: For a full list, please visit https://alkalema.net/ellen.htm.

15. Was the man Jesus Christ also truly God?

The Myth

EGW: NO "The man Christ Jesus was not the Lord God Almighty" (Letter 32, 1899, quoted in the Seventh-day Adventist Bible Commentary, vol. 5, p. 1129).

The Truth

BIBLE : YES "For to us a child is born, to us a son is given, and the government will be on his shoulders. And he will be called Wonderful Counselor, Mighty God, Everlasting Father, Prince of Peace" (Isaiah 9:6).

The Truth

BIBLE: YES "Look, he is coming with the clouds, and 'every eye will see him, even those who pierced him'; and all the peoples of the earth 'will mourn because of him.' So shall it be! Amen. 'I am the Alpha and the Omega,' says the Lord God, 'who is, and who was, and who is to come, the Almighty" (Revelation 1:7-8).

The Truth

BIBLE: YES "Therefore God exalted him [Jesus] to the highest place and gave him the name that is above every name" (Philippians 2:9).

The Lie

Apologist: Both Ellen White and Seventh-day Adventists teach that Jesus was fully God even though He became a real man. We disagree with certain denominations that claim that Jesus was a "lesser God" created by the Father. We maintain that He was one with the Father from eternal ages past and Ellen White continually expressed this view. Now let's look at the quote above in its context: "Christ left His position in the heavenly courts and came to this earth to live the life of human beings. This sacrifice He made in order to show that Satan's charge against God is false--that it is possible for man to obey the laws of God's kingdom. Equal with the Father, honored and adored by the angels, in our behalf Christ humbled Himself, and came to this earth to live a life of lowliness and poverty—to be a man of sorrows and acquainted with grief. Yet the stamp of divinity was upon His humanity. He came as a divine Teacher, to uplift human beings, to increase their physical, mental, and spiritual efficiency. There is no one who can explain the mystery of the incarnation of Christ. Yet we know that He came to this earth and lived as a man among men. The man Christ Jesus was not the Lord God Almighty, yet Christ and the Father are one. The Deity did not sink under the agonizing torture of Calvary, yet it is nonetheless true that "God so loved the world, that he gave his only begotten Son, that whosoever believeth in him should not perish, but have everlasting life." Notice in its context that Ellen White made it quite clear that Jesus was totally equal with the Father when He came to the earth. So, what did she mean then that Jesus wasn't "Lord God Almighty"?

The key word here is "Almighty" (not whether or not Jesus was "truly God" as the heading of this allegation suggests). Before Jesus became a human, He had:

1. Omnipotence
2. Omnipresence
3. Omniscience

When He came to the earth He laid aside:

1. Omnipotence (He said "I can of mine own self do nothing" [He needed the Father] John 5:30.)
2. Omnipresence
3. Omniscience (He said that even He did not know the day or the hour of His own Second Coming, but only the Father knew [Mark 13:32])

Jesus didn't count equality with the Father a thing to be grasped, but for you and me He became a human and was obedient even to the death of the Cross (see Philippians 2:6-8).

Reply to Rebuttal

1. This is another case where EGW got it right in one place and got it wrong in another. The apologists tell us, "Both Ellen White and Seventh-day Adventists teach that Jesus was fully God even though He became a real man." But the truth is, EGW did not regard Christ as fully human

and fully divine. She held to the heretical Arian belief as to Christ's nature – just as did James White, Uriah Smith and many other early Adventists. By making this distinction, EGW makes Jesus a lesser "god" – a "mighty" god – but not "Almighty" God. The Jehovah's Witnesses make this same distinction.

2. How can this be true when Ellen says that Christ was not the "Lord God Almighty?" For whatever reason Ellen White made this statement, it is not Biblical. And if Jesus was just a "man," while on earth, then when did He become "Lord God Almighty?"

If Jesus is not the Lord God Almighty, then the Father cannot be the Lord God Almighty either because Jesus said that He and the Father are one. If the SDAs do not accept Jesus as the Lord God Almighty, then they do not have a Lord God Almighty at all!

Christ was always before and after His incarnation, "the Lord God Almighty." At times as a man, Christ did not display his powers as God and at times He did. He could read the hearts of people, He could tell the future, He could forgive sins, and He could heal the sick. By denying the full deity of Christ, EGW and the apologists contradict the Bible as well as orthodox Christianity, which is the work of antichrist.

Jesus is the Lord God Almighty http://www.truthorfables. com/J-C-Lord-G-Almighty.htm

23. Did Jesus' humanity and divinity die on the cross?

The Myth

EGW: YES "In him dwelleth all the fullness of the Godhead bodily. Men need to understand that Deity suffered and sank under the agonies of Calvary." (Manuscript 44, 1898, and the Seventh-day Adventist Bible Commentary, vol. 7, p. 907).

The Myth

EGW: NO "The Deity did not sink under the agonizing torture of Calvary" (Letter: 1899, quoted in the Seventh-day Adventist Bible Commentary, vol. 5, page 1129).

The Truth

BIBLE: YES "We believe that Jesus died and rose again" (1 Thessalonians 4:14).

NOTE: The Bible repeatedly states that Jesus, the total Person, died on the cross. Four of the first heresies Christianity faced (Appolinarianism, Arianism, Docetism and Nestorianism) denied that Jesus was fully human and fully Divine as a person. Orthodox Christianity maintained the complete unity of Christ's nature in both His life and death. Thus, Ellen White not only contradicted the Bible and orthodox Christianity, but she also contradicted herself.

The Lie

Apologist: Let's look at both Ellen White statements in their context:

> " 'In him dwelleth all the fulness of the God-
> head bodily.' Men need to understand that Deity
> suffered and sank under the agonies of Calvary.
> Yet Jesus Christ whom God gave for the ransom
> of the world purchased the church with His own
> blood. The Majesty of heaven was made to suffer
> at the hands of religious zealots, who claimed to
> be the most enlightened people upon the face of
> the earth."

Here EGW is obviously referring to the Deity of Christ. Although the "fulness of the Godhead" dwelt in Him "bodily" it was the Son only who had to sink in death under the agonies of Calvary; every Christian knows this. Jesus "purchased the church with His own blood." He suffered "at the hands of religious zealots." The Father suffered in a different way: watching His Beloved Son die helplessly on that Cross.

Now the next statement, in its entirety: "There is no one who can explain the mystery of the incarnation of Christ. Yet we know that He came to this earth and lived as a man among men. The man Christ Jesus was not the Lord God Almighty, yet Christ and the Father are one. The Deity did not sink under the agonizing torture of Calvary, yet it is nonetheless true that "God so loved the world, that he gave his only begotten Son, that whosoever believeth in him should not perish, but have everlasting life."

Here she uses the word "Deity" to describe the Godhead— "Christ and the Father" (and the Holy Spirit of course). The Father and Holy Spirit did not "sink" into death like Jesus did. She is clearly saying that although Jesus and the Father are one, the entire Godhead did not sink under the torture of the Cross. Christians understand that when Jesus died, God the Father did not die also. The other two Persons of the Godhead or Trinity were still very much alive; it was the Son who was to die in our stead, not the entire Deity. She is saying, in the context, that although the "Deity" (Father included) did not suffer and die on the Cross, nevertheless God the Father gave His Son to die for us, and what agony that must have been—watching Him die. Here EGW clearly contrasts the role of the Son with the rest of the Godhead, and it is this Godhead to which the word "Deity" refers in this instance. In summary, was Jesus Deity? Yes. Did He sink/die on the Cross? Yes. Are the Father and Holy Spirit Deity? Yes. Did they sink/die on the Cross? No. This is simply a case where a word (like the word "law" for example) is used in different ways.

Reply to Rebuttal

1. The apologists agree with us and the Bible that EGW's first quote was correct, that "Deity" referred to Jesus' Deity that died. "Men need to understand that Deity suffered and sank under the agonies of Calvary" (Manuscript 44,

1898, and the Seventh-day Adventist Bible Commentary, vol. 7, p. 907).

2. The apologists disagree with us that in the second EGW quote that "Deity" did not refer to Jesus but the Godhead. "The Deity did not sink under the agonizing torture of Calvary" (Letter: 1899, quoted in the Seventh-day Adventist Bible Commentary, vol. 5, page 1129). The apologists are putting words in EGW's mouth to cover up her nonbiblical teaching. If indeed EGW meant "the Godhead" instead of Jesus for the term "Deity" she would have made that clear. Isn't that the purpose of the "spirit of prophecy" to make the Bible clear? But here we see once again that EGW and her apologists are the authors of confusion. The Bible fact is clear; Jesus did suffer on the cross and die. Ellen and the apologists are wrong.

3. Ellen White made what she believed clear: that the "Deity" of Jesus did not die but his "humanity" died. This makes EGW and her apologists wrong! EGW: "When the voice of the angel was heard saying, "Thy Father calls thee," He who had said, "I lay down my life, that I might take it again," "Destroy this temple, and in three days I will raise it up," came forth from the grave to life that was in Himself. Deity did not die. Humanity died, but Christ now proclaims over the rent sepulcher of Joseph, "I am the resurrection, and the life." S.D.A. Bible Commentary Vol. 5, page 1113, Chapter Title: Mark paragraph 4. This contradicts EGW's quote "that Deity suffered and sank under the agonies of Calvary."

25. Was the atonement for sin completed at the cross?

The Myth)

EGW: NO "Instead of ... Daniel 8:14 referring to the purifying of the earth, it was now plain that it pointed to the closing work of our High Priest in heaven, the finishing of the atonement, and the preparing of the people to abide the day of His coming" (Testimonies, vol. 1, p. 58).

The Myth)

EGW: NO "Jesus entered the most holy of the heavenly (sanctuary), at the end of the 2,300 days of Daniel 8, in 1844, to make a final atonement for all who could be benefited by His mediation" (Early Writings, p. 253).

The Myth)

EGW: YES "He [Christ] planted the cross between Heaven and earth, and when the Father beheld the sacrifice of His Son, He bowed before it in recognition of its perfection. "It is enough," He said. "The Atonement is complete" (The Review and Herald, Sept. 24, 1901).

The Truth

BIBLE: YES "When he had received the drink, Jesus said, 'It is finished.' With that, he bowed his head and gave up his spirit" (John 19:30).

The Truth

BIBLE: YES "But now apart from law, the righteousness of God has been made known, to which the Law and the Prophets testify. This righteousness from God comes through faith in Jesus to all who believe. There is no difference between Jew and Gentile, for all have sinned and fall short of the glory of God and all are justified freely by his grace through the redemption that came by Christ Jesus. God presented him as a sacrifice of atonement, through the shedding of his blood—to be received by faith" (Romans 3:21-25).

The Truth

BIBLE: YES "Since we have now been justified by his blood, how much more shall we be saved from God's wrath through him! For if, while we were God's enemies, we were reconciled to him through the death of his Son, how much more, having been reconciled, shall we be saved through his life! Not only is this so, but we also boast in God through our Lord Jesus Christ, through whom we have now received reconciliation" (Romans 5:9-11).

The Truth

Bible: Yes "Not only is this so, but we also boast in God through our Lord Jesus Christ, through whom we have now received reconciliation." (Romans 5:11)

NOTE: The Bible totally rejects EGW's idea of the 2,300 days and an investigative judgment in the heavenly sanctuary beginning in 1844. Notice how the Bible texts quoted above were all written less than thirty years after Jesus' resurrection, and all clearly state that Christians living then were already fully justified, redeemed, sanctified and reconciled to God through Christ's death on the cross. As cult-watchers Martin and Barnhouse stated: "The (SDA sanctuary doctrine) is the most colossal, psychological, face-saving phenomenon in religious history! We personally do not believe that there is even a suspicion of a verse in Scripture to sustain such a peculiar position. And we further believe that any effort to establish it is stale, flat, and unprofitable."

The Lie

Apologist: The three Bible texts given are wonderful truths about the gospel, but they do not address (nor refute) the issue in Ellen White's statement at all. Here are four that support what she said: "For since by man came death, by man came also the resurrection of the dead. For as in Adam all die, even so in Christ shall all be made alive." (1 Corinthians 15:21-22 KJV)

"And if Christ be not risen, then is our preach-
ing vain, and your faith is also vain. Yea, and we

are found false witnesses of God; because we have testified of God that he raised up Christ: whom he raised not up, if so be that the dead rise not. For if the dead rise not, then is not Christ raised: And if Christ be not raised, your faith is vain; ye are yet in your sins. Then they also which are fallen asleep in Christ are perished." (1 Corinthians 15:14-18 KJV)

"There is therefore now no condemnation to them which are in Christ Jesus, who walk not after the flesh, but after the Spirit. For the law of the Spirit of life in Christ Jesus hath made me free from the law of sin and death. For what the law could not do, in that it was weak through the flesh, God, sending his own Son in the likeness of sinful flesh, and for sin, condemned sin in the flesh: That the righteousness of the law might be fulfilled in us, who walk not after the flesh, but after the Spirit." (Romans 8:1-4 KJV)

"For if, when we were enemies, we were reconciled to God by the death of his Son, much more, being reconciled, we shall be saved by his life. And not only so, but we also joy in God through our Lord Jesus Christ, by whom we have now received the atonement. Wherefore, as by one man sin entered into the world, and death by sin; and so death passed upon all men, for that all have sinned:

(For until the law sin was in the world: but sin is not imputed when there is no law. Nevertheless, death reigned from Adam to Moses, even over them that had not sinned after the similitude of Adam's transgression, who is the figure of him that was to come. But not as the offence, so also is the free gift. For if through the offence of one many be dead, much more the grace of God, and the gift by grace, which is by one man, Jesus Christ, hath abounded unto many. And not as it was by one that sinned, so is the gift: for the judgment was by one to condemnation, but the free gift is of many offences unto justification. For if by one man's offence death reigned by one; much more they which receive abundance of grace and of the gift of righteousness shall reign in life by one, Jesus Christ.) Therefore as by the offence of one judgment came upon all men to condemnation; even so by the righteousness of one the free gift came upon all men unto justification of life. For as by one man's disobedience many were made sinners, so by the obedience of one shall many be made righteous." (Romans 5:10-19 KJV)

This is exactly what Ellen White was saying, and it is the foundation of Christianity.

Reply to Rebuttal

1. After their long sermon the apologists hoped you had forgotten the contradiction. We ask which of the texts they quote said Jesus was "finishing the atonement" or that a "final atonement" began in 1844 as claimed by EGW? The truth is they did not present a single text to support EGW's claim.

2. The Bible does not tell us, "Jesus entered the most holy in 1844 to make "a final atonement" as claimed by Ellen White. The "final atonement for sins" was made on Calvary 2,000 years ago. God presented him as a sacrifice

of atonement, through faith in his blood (Romans 3:21-25). Christians have been benefited by the "atonement" made at Calvary immediately.

3. The atonement was completed at Calvary and does not give room for a "final atonement" or a "finished atonement" in 1844. EGW and the apologists are saying that Christ's atonement was not complete and final at Calvary. This is simply cult heresy.

26. Does the blood of Christ cancel sin?

The Myth)

EGW: NO "The blood of Christ, while it was to release the repentant sinner from the condemnation of the law, was not to cancel sin ... it will stand in the sanctuary until the final atonement" (Patriarchs and Prophets, p. 357).

The Truth

BIBLE: YES "In him we have [present tense] redemption through his blood, the forgiveness of sins" (Ephesians 1:7).

The Truth

BIBLE: YES "And the blood of Jesus, his Son purifies us from all sin" (1 John 1:7).

The Truth

BIBLE: YES "Blessed are those whose transgressions are forgiven, whose sins are covered. Blessed is the one whose sin the Lord will never count against them" (Romans 4:7-8).

NOTE: To forgive means to pardon, give up all rights to punish, to forever cancel a debt. Jesus did all that for us when He shed His blood for us. The Bible says that forgiven sins are never counted against an individual. However, Ellen White contradicts the Bible by claiming God stores up our sins and later punishes us for them if we do not measure up to His standard before the final atonement. This idea causes millions of SDAs agony as they question whether or not they will be saved.

The Lie

Apologist: This allegation is a re-wording of the last one and again, one needs to study the Investigative Judgment for oneself to understand the validity of it. A few quotes will not shed much light on the issue. The Day of Atonement was a wonderful shadow of the conclusion to God's Plan of Salvation. Any Bible student would be blessed by studying the matter. The texts D&D offer simply say that we have (present tense [if confessed]) redemption and forgiveness and cleansing through Jesus—one of the favorite themes of Ellen White and Adventists. Both Ellen White and Adventists, however, do reject the teaching of "once saved always saved" for the Bible does not teach it.

Reply to Rebuttal

1. The apologists refuse to accept the plain teachings of the
   Bible that sins that are forgiven are forgotten. This has
   nothing to do with the doctrine of "once saved always
   saved." The figurative Day of Atonement was fulfilled at
   Calvary when Jesus was the Lamb slain for our sins and
   the sins of the world. The Day of Atonement was fulfilled
   at the cross just as all the other Annual Holy Days such
   as Passover, Pentecost, Feast of Tabernacles, and so
   forth were fulfilled. SDA's sneer at those who mistakenly
   "keep" the Annual Holy Days, but they themselves
   extend the Day of Atonement past the cross! This
   double-standard only makes sense to deluded believers
   of the false prophet Ellen G. White.

2. Sins are never stored up to be faced in an Investigative
   Judgment. There is not one Bible text telling us that the
   blood of Christ does not cancel confessed sins. Nor is
   there even one Bible text telling us that forgiven sins
   remain in the Sanctuary in Heaven until a final atonement
   in 1844. These are all myths of Ellen G. White.

3. The Bible does not speak of an Investigative Judgment.
   God declared the saints in Hebrews Chapter 11 were
   worthy 2,000 years ago to inherit the City of God. And
   they were not required to go through Ellen G. White's
   nonbiblical 1844 Investigative Judgment.

4. EGW and the apologists are contradicting the gospel of
   Christ by not allowing the blood of Christ to blot out

confessed sins till 1844. Their "new" truth produces a "new" Gospel that merits God's two-fold curse (read Galatians 1:8-9).

27. Are confessed sins transferred to the heavenly sanctuary by the blood of Christ?

The Myth)

EGW: Yes "As the sins of the people were anciently transferred in figure, to the earthly sanctuary by the blood of the sin-offering, so our sins are, in fact, transferred to the heavenly sanctuary by the blood of Christ." (Great Controversy p. 266 1886 Edition).

"As anciently the sins of the people were by faith placed upon the sin offering and through its blood transferred in figure to the earthly sanctuary so in the new covenant the sins of the repentant are by faith placed upon Christ and transferred, in fact, to the heavenly sanctuary." (Great Controversy p. 421 1911 Edition).

The Truth

Bible: No "But if we walk in the light, as he is in the light, we have fellowship with one another, and the blood of Jesus, his Son, purifies us from all sin." (1 John 1:7)

"In him we have redemption through his blood, the forgiveness of sins, in accordance with the riches of God's grace" (Ephesians 1:7)

Note: There is no Scripture to support E. G. White's teaching that confessed sins are transferred to the heavenly sanctuary "by the blood of Christ" in 1886 and she changed it to read, "by faith placed upon Christ" and transferred to the heavenly sanctuary to be dealt with at a later date in an Investigative Judgment. The Bible teaches our confessed sins are completely covered by the blood of the Lamb.

The Lie

Apologist: This allegation also deals with the Investigative Judgment. The texts used to refute Ellen White only support what she had said in the quotes listed.

Reply to Rebuttal

1. The Bible does not teach that our sins are transferred to the Heavenly Sanctuary as taught by Ellen White by the blood of Christ. If you believe we are mistaken, please give us the text.

2. The blood of Christ covers confessed sins, it does not transfer sins anywhere. Sins that are forgiven are blotted out, not saved for a later date of judgment. Again, we challenge you to produce a Bible text contradicting our assertion. Remember how you Seventh-day Adventists have enjoyed offering $1,000 to anyone who can produce

a Bible text showing the Sabbath was changed from Saturday to Sunday? Well, now the shoes on the other foot. Give us one Bible text stating that there was an Investigative Judgment on October 22, 1844. Or give us one Bible text stating that our sins were transferred to the Heavenly Sanctuary in 1844. Or give us one Bible text stating Christ's blood transfers our sins to the Heavenly Sanctuary. Show us the text and we'll give you $1,000. We're waiting. And we'll be waiting till the Lord comes because your Investigative Judgment is a lie, which directly contradicts the Bible.

3. The truth is there is not one Bible writer who ever taught an Investigative Judgment. IJ is an EGW myth believed only by Adventists.

28. Who bears our sins?

The Myth)

EGW: SATAN "It was seen, also, that while the sin offering pointed to Christ as a sacrifice, and the high priest represented Christ as a mediator, the scapegoat typified Satan, the author of sin, upon whom the sins of the truly penitent will finally be placed. ... Christ will place all these sins upon Satan, ... so Satan, ... will at last suffer the full penalty of sin" (Great Controversy, p. 422, 485, 486).

The Truth

BIBLE: JESUS "He himself [Jesus Christ] bore our sins in his body on the cross, so that we might die to sins and live for righteousness; 'by his wounds you have been healed' " (1 Peter 2:24).

The Lie

Apologist: Another Investigative Judgment statement. If one rejects the Investigative Judgment (or the Sabbath, or soul sleep in death, or the Flood for that matter) then that person will be able to find plenty of Ellen White statements that are apparently "wrong." Jesus paid the price for our sins, but Satan is responsible for tempting us to sin. If Jesus wants Satan to pay a price for that, that is His decision. Again, we suggest the reader study the Day of Atonement and read Clifford Goldstein's book on this subject.

Reply to Rebuttal

1. The apologists give no Bible text for God laying confessed sins on Satan at the end of time. Instead, they try to say the Sabbath, Soul Sleep, and the Flood all are linked to the Investigative Judgment. This is pure nonsense! Ellen White is wrong because she does not agree with Scripture – she is not right because she believes in the Investigative Judgment. But her apologists make the IJ the litmus test of "orthodox" belief. The truth is, no Christian has ever taught or believed the Seventh-day Adventist doctrine of

the Investigative Judgment – for the IJ is a cult teaching, it is neither Biblical nor Christian. As soon as we point out EGW's errors in matters of salvation which touch on the IJ, her apologists scurry away like rats from a sinking ship.

2. Our confessed sins are forgiven and blotted out, so they cannot be laid on Satan. Christ is the Christian's sin bearer not Satan.

3. Satan will pay for his sins not the confessed sins of Christians. The unrighteous will pay for their sins. See: Is Jesus or Satan Your Scapegoat?

30. Can we say we are saved right now by Christ's grace?

The Myth)

EGW: NO "Those who accept the Saviour, however sincere their conversion, should never be taught to say or feel that they are saved. ... Those who accept Christ, and in their first confidence say, I am saved, are in danger of trusting to themselves" (Christ's Object Lessons, p. 155).

The Truth

BIBLE: YES "I write these things to you who believe in the name of the Son of God so that you may know that you have eternal life" (1 John 5:13).

The Lie

Apologist: Now let's see the quote in its context:

Peter's fall was not instantaneous but gradual. Self-confidence led him to the belief that he was saved, and step after step was taken in the downward path, until he could deny his Master. Never can we safely put confidence in self or feel, this side of heaven, that we are secure against temptation. Those who accept the Savior, however sincere their conversion, should never be taught to say or to feel that they are saved. This is misleading. Everyone should be taught to cherish hope and faith; but even when we give ourselves to Christ and know that He accepts us, we are not beyond the reach of temptation. God's word declares, "Many shall be purified, and made white, and tried" (Daniel 12:10 KJV). Only he who endures the trial will receive the crown of life (James 1:12). Those who accept Christ, and in their first confidence say, I am saved, are in danger of trusting to themselves. They lose sight of their own weakness and their constant need of divine strength. They are unprepared for Satan's devices, and under temptation many, like Peter, fall into the very depths of sin. We are admonished, "Let him that thinketh he standeth take heed lest he fall" (1 Corinthians 10:12 KJV). Our only safety is in constant distrust of self, and dependence on Christ."

This passage places self where it belongs—in the dust—and shows us our constant need of Jesus. Peter is, as she said, a perfect example of what happens when we declare something to be fact, as if we are out of the range of falling. We can know our relationship is right with God today, but we do not know our weaknesses, or where we could fall and/or turn against God (see Jeremiah 17:9). We can have the assurance that if we were to die today, we would be saved, but to boldly announce that come what may, we are saved is basically "once saved always saved" and that is really what she is warning against.

1 John 5:13 is a beautiful truth as we read above: *"I write these things to you who believe in the name of the Son of God so that you may know that you have eternal life."*

There is nothing wrong with having faith in the fact that we have accepted Jesus' free gift of eternal life. This is the kind of assurance we need. But this text does not say that we should go out and proclaim that we cannot fall, as Peter did. We are warned by Paul to take heed if we think we stand, lest we fall (1 Corinthians 10:12). And Jesus said that some of the "branches" that had "abided" in Him would be cut off and burned if they did not bear fruit (John 15:1-6). In Matthew 7:21-23 Jesus describes a class of people who come to Him, convinced that they are "saved" and to them He says, "I never knew you." They were looking to themselves, which is always a big mistake.

The beauty of all this is not that we doubt God and His ability to save, but rather we doubt ourselves and our ability to do any good thing or overcome sin in our strength. We aren't strong enough to overcome. Only Jesus through us can overcome. This constant awareness of our weaknesses is the only safeguard against presumption and choosing sin over Jesus. Lack of faith in self is one of the most important lessons we can learn.

Reply to Rebuttal

1. Every Christian has the assurance that they are saved when their trust is in Jesus. "He then brought them out and asked, "'Sirs, what must I do to be saved?"' They replied, "'Believe in the Lord Jesus, and you will be saved—you and your household.'" Then they spoke the word of the Lord to him and to all the others in his house" (Acts 16:30-32). "By this gospel you are saved, if you hold firmly to the word I preached to you. Otherwise, you have believed in vain" (1 Corinthians 15:2).

2. EGW takes away the Christian assurance of being saved. She holds the non-biblical doctrine of the Investigative Judgment over their heads and teaches that no one can say they are saved till their name comes up in the Investigative Judgment and God blots out their sins. Of course no one will ever know they are saved till Jesus comes. Because of the Investigative Judgment doctrine, the Adventists cannot say with assurance that they are saved as their confessed sins are still pending.

3. Paul had the assurance that a crown was laid up for him and so can we regardless of EGW's statements that we cannot say we are saved. "Now there is in store for me the crown of righteousness, which the Lord, the righteous Judge, will award to me on that day—and not only to me, but also to all who have longed for his appearing" (2 Timothy 4:8). Jesus gave a woman the assurance that she was saved. "Jesus said to the woman, "Your faith has saved you; go in peace" (Luke 7:50).

The Seventh-day Adventist doctrine of the Investigative Judgment robs their members of the assurance Jesus died on the cross to give to us. It is shameful how this non-Biblical doctrine dreamed up by their false prophet has destroyed their assurance!

34. Can we legitimately say, "I have ceased to sin?"

The Myth)

EGW: YES "Christ died to make it possible for you to cease to sin, and sin is the transgression of the law" (Review and Herald, vol. 71, No. 35, p. 1, August 28, 1894.)

The Myth)

EGW: YES "To be redeemed means to cease from sin" (Review and Herald, vol. 77, No. 39, p. 1, September 25, 1900).

The Myth)

EGW: YES "Those only who through faith in Christ obey all of God's commandments will reach the condition of sinlessness in which Adam lived before his transgression. They testify to their love of Christ by obeying all his precepts" (Manuscript 122, 1901, quoted in the Seventh-day Adventist Bible Commentary, vol. 6, p. 1118).

The Myth)

EGW: YES "To everyone who surrenders fully to God is given the privilege of living without sin, in obedience to the law of heaven. ... God requires of us perfect obedience. We are to purify ourselves, even as he is pure. By keeping his commandments, we are to reveal our love for the Supreme Ruler of the universe" (Review and Herald, September 27, 1906, p. 8).

The Truth

BIBLE: NO "The blood of Jesus, his Son, purifies us from all sin. If we claim to be without sin, we deceive ourselves and the truth is not in us. If we confess our sins, he is faithful and just and will forgive us our sins and purify us from all unrighteousness. If we claim we have not sinned, we make him out to be a liar and his word is not in us" (1 John 1:7-10).

The Truth

BIBLE: NO "For it is by grace you have been saved, through faith and this not from yourselves, it is the gift of God—not by works, so that no one can boast" (Ephesians 2:8-9).

The Lie

Apologist: Note the question raised with this allegation: "Can we legitimately say, 'I have ceased to sin'?" Now considering the evidence presented, let's look at two facts.

1. Not one of the listed Ellen White quotes tells us to say that we have ceased to sin. Ellen White did address this issue in other places though, and here's a sample of what she said: "Those who are really seeking to perfect Christian character will never indulge the thought that they are sinless. Their lives may be irreproachable, they may be living representatives of the truth which they have accepted; but the more they discipline their minds to dwell upon the character of Christ, and the nearer they approach to His divine image, the more clearly will they discern its spotless perfection, and the more deeply will they feel their own defects." And again: "Those who take pains to call attention to their good works, constantly talking of their sinless state and endeavoring to make their religious attainments prominent, are only deceiving their own souls by so doing." (The Sanctified Life, p. 7 & 12)

"But we shall not boast of our holiness. As we have clearer views of Christ's spotlessness and infinite purity, we shall feel as did Daniel, when he beheld the glory of the Lord, and said, "My comeliness was turned in me into corruption." (Selected Messages 3, p. 355)

"Why is it that so many claim to be holy and sinless? It is because they are so far from Christ." (Manuscript 5, 1885)

2. Not one of the Bible texts tells us that we cannot overcome, by God's grace (which is all that the Ellen White quotes were saying).

The first text (1 John 1:8-9) simply says that if we claim we have not sinned God's word has no place in us (and we are in error). Ellen White consistently expressed this view as shown above.

The second text (Ephesians 2:8-9) simply says that we are saved by grace and not works. Again, Ellen White consistently expressed this view:

> "When men learn they cannot earn righteousness by their own merit of works, and they look with firm and entire reliance upon Jesus Christ as their only hope, there will not be so much of self and so little of Jesus. Souls and bodies are defiled and polluted by sin, the heart is estranged from God, yet many are struggling in their own finite strength to win salvation by good works. Jesus, they think, will do some of the saving; they must do the rest. They need to see by faith the righteousness of Christ as their only hope for time and for eternity." (1888 Materials, p. 818)

> "..for nearly every false religion has been based on the same principle—that man can depend upon his own efforts for salvation." (Patriarchs and Prophets, p. 73)

> (see also Testimonies 1, p. 163; Christ's Object Lessons, p. 117; Testimonies to Ministers, pp. 97,

456; Steps to Christ, p. 61; Testimonies 6, p. 372; Evangelism, p. 596; Patriarchs and Prophets, p. 431-2; Acts of the Apostles, p. 298, 553, 563; The Sanctified Life, p.87...)

We have seen that Ellen White fully supported what the Bible taught on salvation by grace through faith. But does the Bible support what she said about overcoming? With no additional commentary, consider the following texts in light of the Ellen White quotes.

"And every man that hath this hope in him purifieth himself, even as he is pure. Whosoever committeth sin transgresseth also the law: for sin is the transgression of the law. And ye know that he was manifested to take away our sins; and in him is no sin. Whosoever abideth in him sinneth not: whosoever sinneth hath not seen him, neither known him." (1 John 3:3-6 KJV)

"This I say then, walk in the Spirit, and ye shall not fulfil the lust of the flesh." (Galatians 5:16 KJV)

"Now unto him that is able to keep you from falling, and to present you faultless before the presence of his glory with exceeding joy." (Jude 24 KJV)

"To him that overcometh will I grant to sit with me in my throne, even as I also overcame, and

am set down with my Father in his throne."
(Revelation 3:21 KJV)

Reply to Rebuttal

1. Because EGW supports salvation by faith and not by works in some places does not excuse her from getting it wrong here by saying, "Those only who through faith in Christ obey all of God's commandments will reach the condition of sinlessness in which Adam lived before his transgression. They testify to their love of Christ by obeying all his precepts" (Manuscript 122, 1901, quoted in the Seventh-day Adventist Bible Commentary, vol. 6, p. 1118).

2. EGW tells us that to attain "sinlessness" like that of Adam before his transgression, it will be by faith in Christ PLUS the works of commandment keeping. The Apostles had faith in Christ and obeyed the commandments, and they were far from being in "the condition of sinlessness." They always needed the Savior's forgiveness.

3. The offspring of Adam will never reach the sinlessness of Adam before his fall. If this were true, we would not need Christ to help us nor would we need a Savior. We are all born with a carnal nature. Even though we have faith in Christ we still have carnal thoughts and temptations from Satan that Adam never experienced before his fall. Jesus is the only sinless one who has ever lived on earth.

37. As a Christian do, I still stand condemned before God?

The Myth)

EGW: YES "At the time the light of health reform dawned upon us, and since that time, the questions have come home every day, 'Am I practicing true temperance in all things? ' 'Is my diet such as will bring me in a position where I can accomplish the greatest amount of good?' If we cannot answer these questions in the affirmative, we stand condemned before God" (Counsels on Diet and Foods, pp. 19, 20).

The Truth

BIBLE: NO "Therefore, there is now no condemnation for those who are in Christ Jesus" (Romans 8:1).

The Truth

BIBLE: NO "For God did not send his Son into the world to condemn the world, but to save the world through him. Whoever believes in him is not condemned" (John 3:17, 18).

The Truth

BIBLE: NO "Very truly I tell you, whoever hears my word and believes him who sent me has eternal life and will not be judged but has crossed over from death to life" (John 5:24).

The Lie

Apologist: D&D correctly show two of the conditions for us to remain out of condemnation. 1) To be "in Christ Jesus" and 2) to "believe" in Christ and the Father. Now let's consider what "in Christ" and "believe" really mean.

Ellen White's statement was about health. The Bible says: "If any man defile the temple of God, him shall God destroy; for the temple of God is holy, which temple ye are" (1 Corinthians 3:17 KJV)

This command is clear. Adventists believe that it is a sin to destroy your body through intemperance (smoking, drinking, destructive eating habits, etc.). This belief is based on the sixth commandment (Thou shalt not kill) as well as a host of other texts like the one above. The Bible definitely promotes Christian health, which is a study all in itself. In light of the above text, would one still be "in Christ" if he or she is intentionally defiling the temple of God. This goes back to the teaching of "once saved always saved" which is not supported by the Bible. Christ Himself taught that there will be those who were at one time "in Christ" but who chose not to maintain that relationship (see John 15:1-5; Matthew 7:21-23; Ezekial 18:24; Revelation 22:19). This relationship is not a one-time decision but must be maintained daily (see 1 Corinthians 15:31).

For many Christians the word "believe" takes in far too little. The Scriptures tell us that even the devils "believe" and tremble (James 2:19), but they are eternally lost. God isn't asking us to merely believe that He is real, and that Jesus was crucified 2,000 years ago. He wants us to believe "every word that proceedeth out of the mouth of God." (Matthew 4:4). Do we believe that Jesus is able to empower us (Jude 24, 1 Corinthians 10:13; 2 Corinthians 10:5; etc.)? If so, then He will; if not, then we don't have faith, and thus do not really "believe" (Matthew 9:29). It's quite simple. It is not for us to decide which portions of God's promises we will believe and which we will doubt. The condition that keeps us out of condemnation is to believe them all.

Reply to Rebuttal

1. The Bible points out our bodies are the temple of the Holy Spirit in 1 Corinthians 3:16. It tells us "anyone that destroys God's temple, God will destroy." This is talking about a person that murders a Christian (God's Temple) and that God will destroy the murder. It is not talking about a person's diet. EGW and the apologists are in error in interpreting this text as dealing with diet.

2. "or the kingdom of God is not a matter of eating and drinking, but of righteousness, peace and joy in the Holy Spirit, because anyone who serves Christ in this way is pleasing to God and receives human approval." (Romans 14:17-18)

3. EGW said, "At the time the light of health reform dawned upon us," that people that did not follow EGW's Health Reform such as not eating meat, sugar, eggs, cheese, pickles and other such items, they would be CONDEMNED BEFORE GOD. People in the Bible have always eaten these products and God never

CONDEMNED them. Christians the last 2000 years have eaten them without God's condemnation. EGW condemns what God has not condemned.

4. God does not condemn Christians, nor does he make it a salvation issue for not following a healthy diet. If God were to do this the majority of SDAs would be lost. They eat eggs, sugar, meat, cheese and many are grossly overweight.

5. It is interesting to note that many non-SDAs use tobacco, coffee, tea, and meat, live longer and reach the age of 100 years and over, than vegetarian SDAs. Perhaps the SDAs are defiling their body temple with the vegetarian Health Foods that the denomination manufactures and markets.

38. Must I be perfect before Christ will accept me?

The Myth)

EGW: YES "From what was shown me, there is a great work to be accomplished for you before you can be accepted in the sight of God" (Testimonies, vol. 2, p. 84).

The Myth)

EGW: YES "You have a great work to do. ... It is impossible for you to be saved as you are" (Testimonies, vol. 2, p. 316).

The Myth)

EGW: YES "As you are, you would mar all heaven. You are uncultivated, unrefined, and unsanctified. There is no place in heaven for such a character as you now possess. ... You are further today from the standard of Christian perfection ... than you were a few months after you had received the truth" (Testimonies, vol. 3, p. 465).

The Truth

BIBLE: NO "Because of his great love for us, God, who is rich in mercy, made us alive with Christ even when we were dead in transgressions -- it is by grace you have been saved" (Ephesians 2:4-5).

The Truth

BIBLE: NO "Accept one another, then, just as Christ accepted you, in order to bring praise to God" (Romans 15:7).

The Truth

BIBLE: NO "God, who knows the heart, showed that he accepted them (the Gentile converts) by giving the Holy Spirit to them, just as he did to us. He made no distinction between us and them, for he purified their hearts by faith" (Acts 15:8-9).

The Lie

Apologist: The question asked was "Must I be perfect before Christ will accept me?" Of the three quotes listed only one has the word "perfection" in it and it says nothing about this being a condition before Christ accepts us. The other two quotes are not talking about perfection but about conditions which will be understood when we look at the quotes in their context.

Ellen White time and time again repeated the fact that we cannot change ourselves, and that we need to come to Christ just as we are for any changes. In fact, she even said we do not need to repent before coming to Christ, for it is He who gives us repentance (see Steps to Christ, p. 14, 15; pocket version). Here she says that many err by thinking that they cannot come to Christ until they repent. Then on page 18 she says, "If you see your sinfulness, do not wait to make yourself better...There is help for us only in God." There are many examples just like this. On that same page she says that if we wait to be "good enough" to come to Jesus, we will never come, but to come as we are. Anyone who has read Ellen White's writings knows her very decisive position on this. In all three cases she is talking to individuals, for their particular situation. We need to see what that situation is before we can know what she meant in the condensed quotes above.

Quote #1 "From what was shown me, there is a great work to be accomplished for you before you can be accepted in the site of God." (Testimonies, vol. 2, p. 84)

She goes on to say to this individual "Self is too prominent. You possess a hasty, passionate temper, and are arbitrary and overbearing in your family." Is Christ abiding in us if self is too prominent? (Can we serve two masters?) Does Christ consider a selfish heart (the essence of Satan's problem) "acceptable" or does this man need a great work to be accomplished for him by Christ? Did she say, "you have a lot of work to do before you can go to Jesus"? No. Who does the work for us? Jesus does. This is in perfect harmony with the Bible. Not one person is "acceptable to Christ" in a selfish, overbearing condition. Only Universalists would debate this point. Did a "great work" need to be done for King Nebuchadnezzar before he was "accepted" by God, or was he just fine when he was setting up an idol and trying to burn God's faithful servants? The "great work" was accomplished for him by God in Daniel chapter 4.

Reply to Rebuttal

Quote 1: EGW "From what was shown me, there is a great work to be accomplished for you before you can be accepted in the sight of God" (Testimonies, vol. 2, p. 84).

1. EGW was reprimanding a Christian man who had a lot of faults. If a person with these faults accepts Christ and is baptized, does God accept them as they are? Yes. This is called justification. Does God still accept a person with faults after they are baptized? Yes. The person may be a long way from having all the Christlike attributes but he is still a Christian.

2. If a person dies with these faults, is he lost or accepted by God? God expects the new Christian to grow in

grace to be Christ like – this is called "progressive sanctification." EGW demonstrated throughout her life that she had some of these very faults she charged this man with and told him there "is a great work to be accomplished for you before you can be accepted in the sight of God." Ellen had faults till the day she died. She has judged herself and, by her own criteria, will not be accepted by God.

3. It is because of our faults that we need Christ as our Savior to help us to be like him. Christians do have un-Christian faults, and God accepts them as they are even as He works with them to be more Christ-like. Look at the faults of the Apostles and every great person in the Bible – their salvation depended upon their acceptance of Christ, not in their achievement of perfection.

4. The apologists use the example of King Nebuchadnezzar as an example of God having to "accomplish a work for him before he could be accepted by God." This is a non-Biblical statement. If Nebuchadnezzar was going to be accepted by God on the basis of his works (his "sanctification"), then he would never be accepted by God. We, and Nebuchadnezzar, are "accepted by God" on the basis of our faith in Christ, not on the basis of our works. The apologists are simply confusing Ellen White's myths with Scripture.

Quote #2 "You have a great work to do. ... It is impossible for you to be saved as you are" (Testimonies, vol. 2, p. 316).

This page (316) clearly lays out what "great work" they (a couple) need to do. Not saving themselves, but quite the opposite: "Now

Jesus invites you to come to Him, and to learn of Him, for He is meek and lowly in heart." When did EGW say they should go to Christ? Now. How much clearer can it be? Listen to this from the same page: "Oh, how important that you see the work to be done for you, before it shall be forever too late!" We do have a work in our salvation: coming to Christ and keeping our eyes on Him; He won't do that for us; He never forces the will. But all growth and victories in our lives come directly from Him. EGW continues: "The promise He has given you is sure, that you will find rest in Him." This hardly sounds like she is instructing them to work their way to perfection before going to Jesus. And the statement "It is impossible for you to be saved as you are" has nothing to do with perfection, but rather supports the biblical teaching that "Today if ye will hear his voice, harden not your hearts" (Hebrews 3:15). It was impossible for the Pharisees to be saved as they were; they needed Christ desperately. It was impossible for Saul/Paul to be saved as he was; he needed Christ desperately. It was impossible for you and me to be saved as we were before Christ, for all of our righteousness is as filthy rags (Isaiah 64:6). This is all in harmony with the Bible.

Reply to Rebuttal

Quote 2: EGW "You have a great work to do. ... It is impossible for you to be saved as you are" (Testimonies, vol. 2, p. 316).

1. The apologist's response to EGW quote 2 by saying EGW is not talking about perfection. If not, what is she talking about? The woman EGW is saying this to a Christian wife

and mother. Ellen is telling her about her shortcomings and that "it is impossible for you to be saved as you are."

2. All Christians have shortcomings. Therefore, according to Ellen White no one can be saved. Our salvation is not in our perfection but in Christ's perfect life and his death to save us.

3. The apologists are using non-Christians such as Saul and the Pharisees and comparing them with Christians. Non-Christians are accepted by God the same way Christians are: by their faith in Jesus Christ. This is called justification by faith.

Quote #3 "As you are, you would mar all heaven. You are uncultivated, unrefined, and unsanctified. There is no place in heaven for such a character as you now possess. ... You are further today from the standard of Christian perfection ... than you were a few months after you had received the truth' (Testimonies, vol. 3, p. 465).

With this quote the subject changes from "Christ accepting me" to "perfection" or victory over sin. Here Ellen White is talking about the transformation of character that comes along after a person has come to Christ. Jesus clearly taught that those who come to Him, and even abide in Him for a while, but do not continue, will ultimately be lost (see John 15:2, 6). Peter talks about those who accept Christ and then turn away. He says that it would have been better for them if they had never known the truth and likens them to a dog returning to his vomit (see 2 Peter 2:20-22). Jesus Himself talked about being "perfect." "Be ye therefore perfect, even as your Father which is in heaven is perfect." (Matthew 5:48 KJV) And Paul: "Finally, brethren, farewell. Be perfect, be of good comfort, be of one mind, live in peace; and the God of love and peace shall be with you." (2 Corinthians 13:11); "Till we all come in the unity of the faith, and of the knowledge of the Son of God, unto a perfect man, unto the measure of the stature of the fulness of Christ" (Ephesians 4:13). "Not as though I had already attained, either were already perfect: but I follow after, if that I may apprehend that for which also I am apprehended of Christ Jesus. . . . Let us therefore, as many as be perfect, be thus minded: and if in anything ye be otherwise minded, God shall reveal even this unto you. (Philippians 3:12, 15 KJV) And James: "But let patience have her perfect work, that ye may be perfect and entire, wanting nothing." (James 1:4 KJV). And Peter: "But the God of all grace, who hath called us unto his eternal glory by Christ Jesus, after that ye have suffered a while, make you perfect, stablish, strengthen, settle you" (1 Peter 5:10 KJV).

Adventist and non-Adventist Christians alike have debated just what is meant by these statements, but none denounce the prophets as being false for using such language. And no one in Adventism, including Ellen White, has ever taught that one must be perfect before coming to Christ. No such statement exists.

The issue here in quote #3 is victory over sin and the perfection of character which Christ (not us) works out in His children. But with this quote—as with the previous 2—if one reads the whole passage, it is clear that Ellen White teaches that the help comes from Christ, and we don't change ourselves.

In light of all EGW says about how one comes to Christ, there is no more reason to attack her on these statements than there is to call Paul a false prophet for admonishing us to "work out your own salvation with fear and trembling" (Philippians 2:12 KJV). We need to look at all Paul said on the subject before we say he contradicts the rest of Scripture.

Reply to Rebuttal

Quote 3: EGW "As you are, you would mar all heaven. You are uncultivated, unrefined, and unsanctified. There is no place in heaven for such a character as you now possess. ... You are further today from the standard of Christian perfection ... than you were a few months after you had received the truth" (Testimonies, vol. 3, p. 465).

1. The apologists point out EGW quote 3 is dealing with perfection after a person has come to Christ. The first and second EGW quote also deals with people that have come to Christ and are Christians with faults.

2. We all have been born with and we have faults in varying degrees as long as we live. We are to be Christ-like in this life as far as possible with the help of God. But we will never attain the perfection of Christ in this life. At the Second Coming the Saints will be resurrected and we will be like Christ. We will not have a carnal nature, and we will be "perfect" in that we are all God created us to be.

3. EGW plays God by confusing sanctification with justification. She makes salvation dependent upon our total sanctification and thus robs her believers of

their assurance of salvation. This is a criminal act on her part. Some Christians have differing views of some aspects of sanctification, but Ellen White's position does not fall into that category. Her doctrines go much farther, are contrary to Scripture, and are an aberration of Christian teachings.

39. Did Jesus enter the most holy place of the heavenly temple before October 22, 1844?

The Myth)

EGW: NO "I was shown that ... the door was opened in the most holy place in the heavenly sanctuary, where the ark is, in which are contained the ten commandments. This door was not opened until the mediation of Jesus was finished in the holy place of the sanctuary in 1844. Then Jesus rose up and shut the door of the holy place, and opened the door into the most holy, and passed within the second veil, where he now stands by the ark" (Early Writings, p. 42).

The Truth

BIBLE: YES "The point of what we are saying is this: We do have such a high priest, who sat down at the right hand of the throne of the Majesty in heaven, and who serves in the sanctuary, the true tabernacle set up by the Lord, not by man" (Hebrews 8:1, 2 written in 60 AD).

The Truth

BIBLE: YES "He did not enter by means of the blood of goats and calves; but he entered the Most Holy Place once for all by his own blood, having obtained eternal redemption" (Hebrews 9:12 written in 60 AD).

NOTE: Both these Bible texts were written in 60 AD, and they both state Jesus was already ministering the in the Most Holy Place of the heavenly sanctuary at least 1,824 years before 1844. Ellen White's 1844 scenario simply contradicts the clearest Scriptures!

The Lie

Apologists: This first text listed says nothing about Jesus being in the Most Holy Place. God's "throne" can be wherever He wants it to be. It is a movable throne (can you imagine God being confined to any one place?), described as having "wheels" (Daniel 7:9). God's presence was not just manifest in the Most Holy Place in the Old Testament either. He was seen by the outer door of the Holy Place with Moses, for one thing (see Exodus 33:8-11). There needs to be some text that declares that God the Father was and is always in the Most Holy Place compartment of the heavenly sanctuary for Ellen White and Adventists to be wrong on this one. No such text exists.

Rebuttal Reply

1. Daniel 7:9 does indeed describe God's throne with wheels. Does the Bible tell us that God rolled his throne from the Most Holy Apartment to the Holy apartment at the ascension to be with Jesus as the apologists suggest? And then God wheeled back into the Most Holy to begin an Investigative Judgment with Jesus in 1844? Of course not! More fiction. – Scripture states after His ascension Jesus "sat down at the right hand of God" (Hebrews 10:12) – which makes a "movable throne" moot! Wherever God's throne was is where Jesus sat down! Furthermore Scripture tells that at Christ's ascension God's throne was in the Most Holy Place, for Jesus entered "behind the curtain" (Hebrews 6:19-20); and that place is called "the Most Holy Place" (Hebrews 9:3); and Scripture specifically tells us Christ entered the Most Holy Place (Hebrews 9:12) – that's the very place where He sat down at the "right hand of God" (Hebrews 10:12). Only a believer in EGW can make a mockery of God's Word by claiming God's throne played musical chairs with Christ until October 22, 1844!

2. EGW points out that the earthly sanctuary was a copy of the heavenly. When did God ever have his throne in the Holy Apartment in the earthly sanctuary? When Jesus ascended to Heaven he sat down on the Father's Throne. The apologists have yet to show God's Throne was ever in the Holy Apartment in the earthly or heavenly Sanctuary.

3. The apologist asks us, "There needs to be some text that declares that God the Father was and is always in the Most Holy Place compartment of the heavenly sanctuary for Ellen White and Adventists to be wrong on this one. No such text exists." Doctrine is not built on what the Bible does not say, but on what it does say. The fact is the Bible never tells us that Jesus was in the Holy Apartment at his ascension as claimed by EGW and her apologists. See our note on #1 above.

4. The New International Version of the Bible renders the second text to say, "Most Holy Place" while the King James simply says, "Holy Place." What does it say in the Greek, though? The Greek in Hebrews 9:12 is very clear that Christ entered both the Holy Place and the Most Holy Place after His ascension and before 70 AD, when the book of Hebrews was written. The Greek literally states: "nor through blood of goats and of calves, but the (His) own blood entered (past tense) once for all into the holies, ("ta hagia" plural – meaning both the holy and most holy place) eternal redemption having found." If you compare with Hebrews 9:25 (which the NIV also translates "the Most Holy Place") in the Greek, there is also "hagia" (plural form) meaning "holies." We can be CERTAIN that "holies" is a clear reference to the Most Holy Place because of the Old Testament context Paul alludes to: that the priest entered the Holy Place every day, but only entered the Most Holy Place once a year on the Day of Atonement (Yom Kippur). Christ entered the "holies" – passed from the Holy Place right on into the

Most Holy Place at His ascension and was seated at the right hand of God on His throne. So our nutty apologists are going to have to admit the SDAs are WRONG!

The only time the book of Hebrews speaks of the second apartment (Most Holy Place) specifically and on its own is in Hebrews 9:3, where it uses the Greek hagia hagion, and translates it correctly as "the holiest of all." In this text it does not say Jesus went there at His ascension; it is simply describing the earthly sanctuary. Nowhere in the entire book of Hebrews is hagia hagion used to tell us where Christ is in heaven. If He entered into the hagia hagion, why didn't Hebrews mention this even once?

It does in Hebrews 9:12 when compared to Hebrews 9:24, as I point out above in both the literal Greek and the English translation as well as the context. Paul used the term "holies," so we'd have the actual progression of Christ traveling through the Holy Place to the Most Holy Place. If Paul had only said: "Christ entered the Most Holy Place" we would have wondered if He dropped in through the roof rather than entering through the curtain! Sorry dudes, you're out of luck with your 1844 nonsense!!

Again, we suggest Clifford Goldstein's book 1844 Made Simple for a more in-depth look at this and other charges against the Investigative Judgment.

Clifford is an attorney trying to be a theologian. His views are the typical cultic SDA response to the non-Biblical support of EGW and her contradictions of Scripture. But then, when you're digging at the bottom of the barrel for some kind of support for a lost cause, what do you dredge up but a LAWYER!

42. What is "the seal of God"?

The Myth

EGW: SABBATH "The enemies of God's law, from the ministers down to the least among them, have a new conception of truth and duty. Too late they see that the Sabbath of the fourth commandment is the seal of the living God" (Great Controversy, p. 640).

The Truth

BIBLE: HOLY SPIRIT "You were marked in him with a seal, the promised Holy Spirit" (Ephesians 1:13).

The Truth

BIBLE: HOLY SPIRIT "Do not grieve the Holy Spirit of God with whom you were sealed for the day of redemption" (Ephesians 4:30).

NOTE: This is a crucial contradiction. The Bible is certain that God's seal is the Holy Spirit. But EGW denies this Bible truth, claiming that the seventh day Sabbath is God's seal. Thus Sabbath-keeping is promoted as the great determiner of who is lost and who is saved.

In this, EGW proclaims that it is the Sabbath which saves, rather than Jesus Christ who saves! This is heresy, claiming salvation by works. EGW makes the Sabbath the greatest commandment of all. James 2: tells if you offend in one point of the law (adultery, murder,) you are guilty of all. Halo?

The Lie

Apologist: Most Bible translations other than NIV have Ephesians 1:13 in agreement with 4:30 on the fact that the Holy Spirit does the sealing. Adventists use these same texts all the time in Bible studies, for they help explain what the seal really is and Who does the sealing. God's seal involves the Holy Spirit in our hearts, Christ's character formed within, and God's name in our "foreheads"/minds (see Ephesians 1:13 & 4:30; Colossians 1:27; Revelation 7:3 & 14:1). When the mark of the beast is enforced, those who have the above three characteristics will choose to obey the Word of God rather than the laws of men even when faced with death (see Isaiah 24:1-6; Psalm 119:126; Revelation 14:12 & 12:11). They will keep God's Sabbath day holy. The Seal of God—like the Investigative Judgment—is a Bible study all in itself. The texts listed here do not disprove the belief that the Sabbath is God's seal in the final days. Ellen White summed up the relationship of the Holy Spirit and the seal of God this way:

"The sanctification of the Spirit signalizes the difference between those who have the seal of God and those who keep a spurious rest day." Bible Commentary, Vol. 7, p. 980.

Reply to Rebuttal

1. Did you notice that the apologists could not give a text that tells us that the Seal of God is Sabbath keeping for Christians?

2. When the apologists cannot support from the Bible that "the seal of God is Sabbath keeping" they go to EGW for their support. This is called circular reasoning. In other words, the apologists are using EGW as interpreter of Scripture. Shame on any person that accepts this cultic reasoning. EGW: "The sanctification of the Spirit signalizes the difference between those who have the seal of God and those who keep a spurious rest day" (Bible Commentary, Vol. 7, p. 980).

45. Is it a sin to be sick?

The Myth)

EGW: YES "It is a sin to be sick; for all sickness is the result of transgression" (Counsels on Health, p. 37).

The Truth

BIBLE: NO "So Satan went out from the presence of the Lord and afflicted Job with painful sores from the soles of his feet to the top of his head. ... In all this, Job did not sin" (Job 2:7, 10).

NOTE: It is a matter of record that Ellen White was sick a lot --does that mean she sinned a lot?

The Lie

Apologist: Here is the very next sentence after the above Ellen White quote.

> "Many are suffering in consequence of the transgression of their parents. They cannot be censured for their parents' sin" (Counsels on Health, p. 37)

Here we clear up any notion that everyone who gets sick is just paying the price for their own sins. Many things are handed down and we have no control of that. If our parents and ancestors abuse their health (a pregnant mother on drugs or alcohol, for example) we end up being affected by it, fair or not. This is all still the result of violating God's laws of health and nature. In fact, there would BE NO SICKNESS if Adam and Eve hadn't sinned in the first place. God doesn't invent sickness; it is the result of living in a sinful world and is amplified by our own unhealthful practices. This is what she meant by calling it "sin." As we saw in her very next sentence, she didn't mean that by getting sick one has then and there committed a sin. All of the human health problems are the result of an accumulation of sins and violations of the health laws, no honest person can deny that.

The listed Bible text (Job 2:7, 10) shows Satan inflicting Job with sores, and obviously this was not Job's fault. If Ellen White were saying what D&D are trying to prove that she's saying, then this text (along with many others) would prove her wrong; but she's simply not saying that.

D&D add "It is a matter of record that Ellen White was sick a lot –does that mean she sinned a lot?" Much of Ellen White's poor health conditions were the result of that tragic and nearly fatal accident as a child, but even for the other times when she was sick, we need to understand what she was saying (by reading the next sentence) before we call her a hypocrite or accuse her of contradicting the Bible.

Reply to Rebuttal

1. EGW does say, "It is a sin to be sick for all sickness is the result of transgression." God never tells us that being sick is a sin, regardless of if we inherited weakness from our parents genes or bad health habit.
2. She goes on to say they should *not be censored* for their parent's sin. Why should people be censored for their parent's sins? God does not say they are sinning because they are sick.
3. Never-the –less EGW holds people guilty of sinning for being sick because of their inherited health problems, not their parent's sins.
4. *No one is ever held guilty by god for their parent's sinful habits or diseases they may have passed on to their children at birth.*

46. Will God prevent the wicked from killing his people who refuse to receive the mark of the beast?

The Myth)

EGW YES "God would not suffer (allow) the wicked to destroy those who were expecting translations and who would not bow to the decree of the beast or receive his mark. I saw that if the wicked were permitted to slay the saints, Satan and all his evil host and all who hate God, would be gratified. ... The swords that were raised to kill God's people broke and fell powerless as a straw. Angels of God shielded the saints" (Early Writings, pp. 284, 285).

The Truth

BIBLE: NO "I saw the souls of those who had been beheaded because of their testimony for Jesus and because of the word of God. They had not worshipped the beast or his image and had not received his mark on their foreheads or their hands. They came to life and reigned with Christ a thousand years" (Revelation 20:4).

The Lie

Apologist: This has less to do with "contradictions" and more to do with eschatology. Adventists believe in a close of probation. Once probation closes then the death of God's faithful ones would serve no purpose, for no one lost after their probation closes will go to the other side and be saved (by the very definition of "probation"). The blood of martyrs would after that point sow no seed for the gospel (see Great Controversy, 634). Thus, the Ellen White statement that D&D quote (Early Writings, 284,285) about God not allowing His faithful ones to be slain by the wicked is correct, for this is after the close of probation. The martyrs portrayed in the listed Bible text (Rev. 20:4) are those who are killed before the close of probation (see Manuscript Releases 20, p. 14).

Reply to Rebuttal

1. The Bible never uses the term "probation." This is a non-biblical term used by Ellen White and Joseph Smith. Christians are not nor have they ever been "on probation."
2. God does not tell us that before Jesus returns that the wicked will attack the saints and attempt to put them to death for not receiving the MARK OF THE BEAST (Sunday keeping). This is another of EGW'S myths.
3. Revelation 20:4, tells us that the saints were beheaded for the Testimony of Jesus and his word and not for Sunday keeping. This has nothing to do with before or after probation closes -- the term is not mentioned.
4. John sees those that were beheaded for not worshipping the Beast and its image and EGW sees those that do not worship the Beast being protected by angels and

not dying. Which is the true story? The Bible of course has the truth, not the ravings of a false prophet and her apologists.

49. Will we know the exact day and hour of Christ's coming?

The Myth)

EGW: YES "As God has shown me in holy vision ... we heard the voice of God like many waters, which gave us the day and hour of Jesus' coming" (Early Writings, pp. 15, 34, 285).

The Truth

BIBLE: NO "Therefore, keep watch, because you do not know the day or the hour" (Matthew 25:13).

The Truth

BIBLE: NO "About that day or hour no one knows, not even the angles in heaven, nor the Son, but only the Father" (Matthew 24:36).

The Lie

Apologist: Jesus Himself didn't know the "day or the hour" when He was on the earth (Matt. 24:36), but He certainly does now. Ellen White in the above quote is simply stating that God will reveal this information to His "sealed" servants during the time of trouble to give them comfort that their deliverance is near. There are no Bible texts that say the redeemed will never know the day and the hour of the Second Coming after the close of probation.

Reply to Rebuttal

1. The apologists tell us that there are no Bible texts that tell us "the redeemed will never know the day and hour of the Second Coming." Yes, there is! "Therefore keep watch, because you do not know on what day your Lord will come. But understand this: If the owner of the house had known at what time of night the thief was coming, he would have kept watch and would not have let his house be broken into. So you also must be ready, because the Son of Man will come at an hour when you do not expect him. 45 "Who then is the faithful and wise servant, whom the master has put in charge of the servants in his household to give them their food at the proper time?" (Matthew 24:42-45)

2. God has never shown any prophet the day and hour of His return. This proves EGW is a false prophet.

ELLEN G. WHITE'S ADDITIONS TO THE HOLY BIBLE[18]

By Robert K. Sanders

The EGW Apologists did not reply to Additions because they believe it is proper for prophets to add to the teachings of our Bible.

1. Did Satan repent after his fall?

EGW: YES "After Satan was shut out of heaven, with those who fell with him, he realized that he lost all the purity and glory of heaven forever. Then he repented and wished to be reinstated in heaven. He was willing to take his proper place, or any place that might be assigned him. ... He and his follower repented, wept and implored to be taken back into the favor of God. But no, their sin their hate, their envy and jealousy, had been so great that God could not blot it out. It must remain to receive its final punishment" (Spiritual Gifts, vol. 1, p. 18, 19).

Note: Not Biblical. But, in Matthew 18:21-22, Jesus told Peter to forgive seventy times seven (490 times). If Ellen White was right, then it is strange that God expected more from Peter than He was willing to do Himself by refusing to forgive Satan! Wouldn't Christ have been willing to die in Satan's place -- had Satan repented? Is God really unmerciful and unforgiving?

2. Adam was more than twice as tall as men today.

EGW: Yes "As Adam came forth from the hand of his Creator.... He was more than twice as tall as men now living upon the earth....Eve was not quite as tall as Adam. Her head reached a little above his shoulders." (Spiritual Gifts, Vol. III p. 34).

> "Adam's height was much greater than that of men who now inhabit the earth. Eve was somewhat less in stature;" (Patriarchs and Prophets p. 45).

Note: Not Biblical. The Bible does not tell us the height of Adam and Eve, but Ellen does not leave us in doubt as to their height.

3. In the fires of hell, do the wicked feel pain as long as there is one piece of flesh left?

EGW: Yes "I saw that some were quickly destroyed, while others suffered longer. ... Some were many days consuming, and just as long as there was a portion of them unconsumed, all the sense of suffering was there" (Spiritual Gifts, vol. 1, p. 217).

Note: Not Biblical. What if their brain is consumed first; will they still feel pain? Can a finger feel pain after the rest of the body is destroyed? Where is a Bible text to support this error?

4. Did Judas have a conviction to confess his sin?

EGW: 1898 Yes "When the Saviour's hands were bathing those soiled feet, and wiping them with the towel, the heart of Judas thrilled through and through with the impulse then and there to confess his sin." (Desire of Ages p. 645).

EGW: 1902 No "As Christ celebrated this ordinance with His disciples, conviction came to the hearts of all save Judas." (Evangelism p. 275).

Note: Not Biblical. Mrs. White said yes in 1898 and God and Ellen changed their minds in 1902 and said no. This kind of inspiration is very hard to keep up with. I am thankful that the prophets of the Bible did not have this problem.

5. Was John cast into a cauldron of boiling oil before being banished to the Isle of Patmos?

EGW: Yes " John was cast into a caldron of boiling oil; but the Lord preserved the life of His faithful servant even as he preserved the three Hebrews in the fiery furnace. By the emperor's decree John was banished to the Isle of Patmos" (Acts of the Apostles p. 570).

Note: Not Biblical: The miracles of life preservation have been recorded in Scripture to glorify God and to give us confidence in God's mercies. It seems strange that John chose not to glorify God with this miracle as Paul did when God delivered him and as recorded in Daniel of the fiery furnace and Daniel in the Lion's den. If this miracle happened to me, being delivered from boiling oil, I would be shouting it from the housetops. It took God 2000 years to get this information to us by way of Ellen G. White. Why was it important for the Seventh-day Adventist Church to know about this miracle and not to have it recorded in Scripture for the encouragement of the Saints that went through persecutions? To believe this, one must have tremendous faith or be a deluded individual.

6. The Herod mistake and cover-up.

E. G. White was under the impression that the Herod that took part in Jesus' trial was the same Herod that took the life of James. She did not realize that it was Herod Antipas who took part in Jesus' trial and Herod Agrippa I who put James to death. This mistake was due to her ignorance of the Bible and Bible history.

Writing under inspiration; E. G. White wrote in 1858 that, "Herod's heart grew still harder, and when he heard that JESUS had arisen, he was not much troubled. He took the life of James; and when he saw that this pleased the Jews, he took Peter also, intending to put him to death." (Spiritual Gifts Vol 1, p.71).

Note: The cover-up: This error was never corrected in the revisions of Early Writings. But when the error was discovered, the authors tried to fix it by a footnote on page 185 of Early writings saying it was, "the same Herodian spirit only in another personality." Notice Ellen was talking under inspiration about an individual, Herod, not the spirit of an individual or their attributes. Jesus certainly knew the difference between the Herod's and the reason Ellen did not, was that she was not inspired and did not have the gift of prophecy.

7. John the Baptist knew that he was going to die.

EGW: Yes "He knew that when Jesus should establish himself as a teacher, he must die" (Spiritual Gifts Vol. 1, p. 29).

Note: Not Biblical. There is no Bible record of John knowing when he was going to die.

8. Mary the sister of Martha and Lazarus, was Mary Magdalene, and she was led into sin by Simon.

EGW: Yes The Feast At Simons' House. "Simon had led into sin the woman he now despised. "It was Mary who poured upon His head the precious anointing oil, and bathed His feet with her tears. Mary was first at the tomb after the resurrection." (Desire of Ages p. 566,568).

Note: Mary, the sister of LAZARUS is never identified as Mary Magdalene, nor is it ever suggested from the Bible that Simon led Mary into sin and despised her.

9. Jesus' brothers were older than he and they were the sons of Joseph and sided with the rabbis.

EGW: Yes "All this displeased His brothers. Being older than Jesus, they felt that He should be under their dictation. His brothers, as the sons of Joseph were called, sided with the rabbis. They insisted that the traditions must be heeded, as if they were the requirements of God." (Desire of Ages, p.86,87.)

Note: Not Biblical. Ellen G. White adds to the Bible the same way that Joseph Smith does in the "Book of Mormon." How can Adventist claim that the Bible is the source of their faith and accept this as "the truth," and do it with a straight face?

10. Angels need a gold card to get into and out of heaven.

EGW: Yes "All angels that are commissioned to visit earth hold a golden card, which they present to the angels at the gates of the city." (Early Writings p. 39).

Note: Not Biblical. If this statement came from Joseph Smith, would you accept it? No, because it is not found in the Bible. Then using the same principle for defining your faith how can you believe EGW's nonsense as truth? Does God who can number the hairs on our head, need a gold card to identify the angels? Why have angels at the gate when an ATM machine would work just as well?

11. Ellen G. White the only prophet given wings while in vision.

EGW: Yes "The Lord has given me a view of other worlds. Wings were given me, and an angel attended me from the city to a place that was bright and glorious." (Early Writings p. 39).

Note: Not Biblical. No Bible prophet was ever given wings at any time. Why were wings given to Ellen White in her vision? In vision they would not be necessary for travel. She certainly had a vivid imagination.

12. Marriages are to be discouraged.

EGW: Yes In 1885 EGW wrote, "In this age of the world, as the scenes of earth's history are soon to close and we are about to enter upon the time of trouble such as never was, the fewer the marriages contracted, the better for all, both men and women." 5 Testimonies, p. 366.

Also in 1885, "The time has come when, in one sense, they that have wives be as though they had none." (Ellen G. White, MS 34, The White Estate, 1885. Quoted in "Are Seventh-Day Adventists False Prophets?" p.29 by Wallace D. Slattery).

Note: Not Biblical. To my knowledge Adventist Pastors today have not been discouraging any marriages. This is evident that they do not accept this teaching. The Bible was written for us and it does not ever discourage Christian marriages. The Bible does speak about marriage in the last days, calling those that forbid marriages, "liars."

> "The Spirit clearly says that in later times some will abandon the faith and follow deceiving spirits and things taught by demons. Such teachings come through hypocritical liars, whose consciences have been seared as with a hot iron They forbid people to marry and order them to abstain from certain foods, which God created to be received with thanksgiving by those who believe and who know the truth" (1 Timothy 4:1-3).

13. Do we have power in ourselves?

EGW: No 1862 "If Satan can so befog and deceive the human mind as to lead mortals to think that there is an inherent power in themselves to accomplish great and good works, they cease to rely upon God to do for them that which they think there is power in themselves to do" (1 Testimony, p. 294).

EGW: Yes 1870 "We all have a warfare before us, and must stand in a position to resist the temptations of Satan; and we want to know that we possess the power in ourselves to do this (Councils on Diet and Foods, p.169).

14. Is tithe paying a pre-requisite for praying for the sick?

EGW: Yes "Prayer For the Sick ¾ We should first find out if the sick one has been withholding tithes or has made trouble in the church" (Healthful Living, p. 237).

Note: Not Biblical. This teaching would prohibit praying for sick non-Christian friends and relatives as well as Christians of other faiths that are sick that do not believe tithing is a requirement for the Christian Church. I could not find any example of Jesus or the Apostles checking on anyone's tithing performance before they healed them. I have never seen any Adventist Pastor follow Ellen's ("inspired?") on this teaching. If you really believe that Ellen G. White is a prophetess, then you will have to check and see if the sick is a tithe payer before you pray for them. Put your faith to the test, are you going to follow Jesus or Ellen?

15. The redeemed are to fill the vacancies in heaven left by Satan and his angels.

EGW: Yes "The vacancies made in heaven by the fall of Satan and his angels will be filled by the redeemed of the Lord" (Watchman Nov. 78, 1905).

> "It was God's purpose to repopulate Heaven with the human race, if after the test and trial they proved to be loyal to Him" (Signs of the Times,

May 29, 1909).

Note: Not Biblical. The Bible never mentions that the redeemed will take the place of Satan and the fallen Angels nor does Scripture say that it is God's purpose to repopulate heaven with the human race. The Scripture does say that God is creating a New Earth for the redeemed (see Revelation 21:1).

SEVENTH-DAY ADVENTIST'S CLAIM

Seventh-day Adventist claim to be people of the Bible and that their beliefs are supported by Scripture. They reject the Roman Catholic Church beliefs such as, praying to Mary and the saints, the confessional, rosary, holy water, the Pope as head of the church, etc. They reject Joseph Smith and his book of Mormon; they reject Mary Baker Eddy and her book Science and Health with Keys to Scripture. They reject the Jehovah's Witnesses, which have the Watchtower to guide them. SDAs reject all beliefs that cannot be supported by the Bible. The paradox is, that the church accepts Ellen White's additions to the Bible and her contradictions without question. And then, like any other cult, expects members to do likewise. These additions to Scripture may seem too trivial to even mention. However, the church insists all these additions and contradictions came straight from God, thus making God a part of their deception.

HOW IS THIS POSSIBLE?

The Seventh-day Adventist Church tell us:

> "The writings of Mrs. E. G. White were never de-
> signed to be an addition to the canon of Scripture.
> They are, never-the less, the messages of God to
> the remnant church and should be received as
> such as were the messages of the prophets of old.
> As Samuel was a prophet to Israel in his day, as
> Jeremiah was a prophet to Israel in the days of
> the captivity, as John the Baptist came as a spe-
> cial messenger of the Lord to prepare the way
> for Christ's appearing, so we believe that Mrs.
> White was a prophet to the Church of Christ to-
> day. And the same as the messages of the proph-
> ets were received in olden times, so her messages
> should be received at the present time" (Review
> and Herald, October 4, 1928).

Note: Christians accept the writing of the prophets, Samuel,
Jeremiah, as inspired by God and their writings as Holy Scripture.
To follow what the SDA Church tells its members, then those
who believe that E. G. White is inspired would have to regard her
writings as Scripture (the same way) as they do the Bible prophets.
But then the church tells them her writings are not "an addition to
the canon of Scripture!" Does this confuse you? If you understand
how, it is possible, please explain it to me!

Did E. G. White claim infallibility for the Testimonies?

Yes.

"Yet, now when I send you a testimony of warning and reproof, many of you declare it to be merely the opinion of Sister White. You thereby insulted the Spirit of God" (Testimonies 5, p. 64).

"In these letters which I write, in the testimonies I bear, I am presenting to you that which the Lord has presented to me. I do not write one article in the paper expressing merely my own ideas. They are what God has opened before me in vision--the precious rays of light shining from the throne" (Testimonies 5 p. 67).

"If you lessen the confidence of God's people in the testimonies He has sent them, you are rebelling against God as were Korah, Dathan, and Abriam" (Testimonies 5 p. 66).

"The Testimonies are of the Spirit of God, or of the devil. In arraying yourself against the servants of God you are doing a work either for God or for the devil" (Testimonies 4 p. 230).

Resources

Books and Movies about Heaven

1. *Heaven is For Real: A Little Boy's Astounding Story of His Trip to Heaven and Back* by Todd Burpo and Lynn Vincent. Adult and Children's books. It's also a movie.
2. *90 Minutes in Heaven* by Don Piper and Cecil Murphey. Book and Movie
3. *Glimpses of Heaven* by Trudy Harris, RN, Book
4. *The Case for Heaven* by Lee Strobel. Book and Movie
5. *After Death.* Movie

Websites

https://answeringadventism.com/
https://alkalema.net/ellen.htm
https://www.nonsda.org/egw/egw36.shtml

Notes

1. Lucinda Burdick as quoted in Miles Grant, *An Examination of Mrs. Ellen White's Visions* (Advent Christian Publication Society, 1877).
2. American Christian Ministries, "DOUG BATCHELOR Understanding Ellen White #Dougbatchelor #Amazingfacts," August 23, 2023, https://www.youtube.com/watch?v=CJKd4zdYqDM.
3. Ellen Gould White, *To Be Like Jesus"* (Hagerstown, MD: Review and Herald Publishing Association, 2004).
4. Dalton D. Baldwin, Ph.D., *Openness for Renewal without Destructive Pluralism: The Dilemma of Doctrinal Dissent* (Pres of Benjamin Lindsey, 1846), 31-32.
5. Ellen Gould White, *Testimonies for the Church*, vol. 1 (Pacific Press Publishing Association, 1885), 116.1.
6. Ellen G. White, *The Great Controversy – Ellen G. White Writings*. m.egwwritings.org. Chapter 28.
7. Ellen G. White. *Counsels on Diet and Foods* (Hagerstown, MD: Review and Herald, 1938), 5.
8. Corrie Schoroder, "Seventh Day Adventist," UCSB Holocaust Oral History Project, March 2002, https://holocaust.projects.history.ucsb.edu/Research/Proseminar/corrieschroder.htm.

9. "Erbkrank" R. Sulzmann, *Gegenwarts-Frage*, vol. 9, nr.1, 1934, p.8, quoted by: Sicher, "Seventh-day Adventist Publications and the Nazi Temptation," 19.

10. Sulzmann, *Gegenwarts-Frage*.

11. Schoroder, "Seventh Day Adventist." Mr. Blaich does not say who this quote is from, but it seems to be from G.W. Schubert to the General Conference Committee, Feb. 7, 1937. Or it is from the Circular to the Conference Presidents of the East German Union, Mar. 27, 1940. Blaich, "Divided Loyalties," 45.

12. Schoroder, "Seventh Day Adventist." "An unsere Gemeindeglieder in Deutschland," Der Adventbote, vol. 39, nr. 17, August 15, 1933, pp. 1-4. quoted by: Sicher, "Seventh-day Adventist Publications and The Nazi Temptation," 15.

13. Schoroder, "Seventh Day Adventist."

14. CBN. "Trump: Not Sorry for Attack on Carson's Adventist Faith." https://www.youtube.com/watch?v=VQQd0DUB7JE.

15. Ellen G. White, *The Great Controversy* (Pacific Press Publishing Association, 2009), 605-606.

16. "The SDA System of Fear | Armchair Theologian." Accessed October 29, 2024. https://actheologian.com/2016/08/22/the-sda-system-of-fear/.

17. Robert K. Sanders." ELLEN G. WHITE CONTRADICTS the BIBLE OVER 50 TIMES." 2006. https://alkalema.net/ellen.htm.

18. Robert K. Sanders." ELLEN G. WHITE'S ADDITIONS TO THE HOLY BIBLE." 2006. https://alkalema.net/ellen.htm.